DJ Techniques

Printed and bound in Great Britain by Antony Rowe Limited, Chippenham, Wiltshire

Published in the UK by SMT, an imprint of Sanctuary Publishing Limited, Sanctuary House, 45-53 Sinclair Road, London W14 0NS, United Kingdom

www.sanctuarypublishing.com

ISBN: 1-84492-027-5

DJ Techniques

Tom Frederikse and David Sloly

smt

ACKNOWLEDGEMENTS

David

Thanks to Annette Sedgwick for putting up with late-night keyboard tapping and still loving me; Karen and Tom Larson for the use of their yard; my folks, Jean and Karl, for the support they gave; my brother Mark for knowing so much about music; my good friend Dr Paul Thomas (you are a star); Luke Smith, a true knight of wrongness; Lee Corbin; Rob and Jules at Point-Blank; and, finally, that little white island of joy, Ibiza.

Tom

Thanks a million yet again to Rob for absolutely everything; several huge thanks to Jules for all the music (you're fabulous, babe); thanks to Iain and Alan at Sanctuary Publishing for believing and for having wickedly quiet confidence; thanks to Lewis Brangwyn for your fabulous (and unbelievably fast) work; and, most of all, thanks to Mishy, Molly, Casey and Ruby (the very best people in the world).

CONTENTS

CD CONTENTS

The enclosed instructional audio CD contains suitable tunes for learning how to mix. These tunes can be mixed on CD decks or downloaded onto a PC for digital mixing.

1 **'Hyponitized' (130bpm)**
Four-on-the-floor, funky vocal house, very easy to mix due to the distinguishable sections.

2 **'Bak 2 Luv' (128bpm)**
Four-on-the-floor, easy intro for beat mixing with long drums-only sections.

3 **'Wake Up' (105bpm)**
Try to isolate a few sounds in this track for practising scratch techniques over other hip-hop beats.

4 **'Hear This' (135bpm)**
Reggae influenced. Try mixing this track over a drums-only section in a house track, or mixing a slow-tempo reggae track with a bpm speed of half of this one. (Note: This track starts on the off-beat.)

5 **'Give It To Me' (130bpm)**
This is a good instrumental for mixing a cappellas or MCing over.

6 **'Give It To Me' (with early breakdown, 130bpm)**
Garage beat. Try also beat-mixing sections of this track over a four-on-the-floor beat.

7 **'Step On' (98bpm)**
This has a difficult intro to mix; try to mix in after 16 bars.

8 **'Wake Up' (a cappella, 105bpm)**
Varispeed this up and change the pitch, and mix over a selection of instrumentals.

FOREWORD

This is a book about modern DJing, but in the classic and traditional sense, so the material within is timeless and will never require updating. The book begins with the absolute basics for absolute beginners but quite quickly gets to the most difficult tricks which might take even well-experienced DJs some time to master, if they haven't already.

While it is nigh-on impossible to generalise about DJs, the authors nevertheless managed to find some universal truths that any DJ can relate to. Founded on years of close observation of thousands of DJs, in the UK and around the world, Tom and David identify the fundamentals that bind all DJs and turntablists, and offer steps to build on it with innovation and inspiration.

The authors are enormous music fans and fixtures in the dance music business. They were midwives at the birth of modern dance music in the '80s and they've stayed close to the heart of the scene right through. With experience ranging from hit-record production and remixing to producing and presenting the radio and video face of music, they are perfectly placed to bring it all together into one indispensable source. (The only wonder is how they found the time to do it.)

Everybody needs a little help now and then, and this book provides a little something for everyone. Part textbook, part reference and part manifesto, this is one to keep close at hand at all times – and it's no accident that it fits snugly into a record box. Enjoy.

Rob Cowan
London
July 2003

1 DJ CULTURE

'If you are going to be serious as a DJ then hire an accountant that you can really trust; by that I mean trust entirely to look after all your DJ business interests.' *Alex P, DJ*

In the heady days of the late 1970s, when punk rock was at its peak, legend has it that every chatty cab driver in London would be quick to confess to his passenger that he played guitar. Now, it seems, nearly 30 years later, they're all DJs.

From the bad old days when every party or club featured an unemployed plumber behind a single record player set up on a cardboard box repeatedly playing the same dozen or so seven-inch singles (each one with an annoying skip), the modern DJ has risen so far as to stand proudly among the biggest icons of our time. From lowly beginnings, we've made it. Man.

And made it big, too: while live bands struggle to get gigs which pay barely enough to leave each member with his cab fare home, many DJs make a healthy living doing four sets a week, and some DJs – the 'Superstar DJs' – can make 'house money' (that's enough to buy a house, honest!) for a single set.

DJing can seem dangerously close to money for nothing (and chicks for free, of course), but, as so often happens in life, becoming an 'overnight success' inevitably takes quite a long time.

Musicians

DJs are now arguably the most important musicians of our time. It is they who choose what we hear at the club, at the party, on the radio and even on TV. Straight musicians (who aren't DJs) tend to migrate towards us to figure out what it is they're missing. There is hardly an act in the charts that doesn't either feature a DJ or isn't closely connected to one.

DJs mix the music we listen to and all the while put their own identity stamp on it. Most of the top music producers of the last few years have been DJs – and those who aren't have DJ partners. The record companies, too, are well aware of DJ culture, and they've got fingers in all the pies. DJs run some of the biggest record labels, and they control the output of the music business. So, as a DJ, you're well set up to mix and make your records and to sign them to other DJs sitting in the record-executive chair. As a DJ in the 21st century, the world – plus the club, the studio, the boardroom and the bedroom – is your oyster.

The Vibe: A Long, Strange Trip

Deciding to become a DJ, however, is not a career choice, any more than deciding to have dinner is a lifestyle option. DJing tends to be something that DJs have to do.

Deciding to become a DJ is the start of an adventure into music. The whole essence of being a DJ is to become part of the music itself, and to achieve this you have to know music, live music and breathe music.

Music, of course, breaks down into many different types, each of which breaks down into yet more types. During your life as a DJ, it can seem that music is subdividing and multiplying like some kind of biological weapon.

Some DJs specialise in being able to play and mix many different styles of music in one night – or even one set. (This can be useful if you also play functions that are attended by a wide assortment of people, such as a wedding or a party.) Other DJs prefer to mix and play from just one genre of music. The benefit to this approach is that they can hone their skills in that style and make a name for themselves within a select group.

At some point (and now is as good a time as any), you will need to decide what style or genre (or

A top DJ performs at the Ministry Of Sound

combination) of music you're going to play. It's usually best – and certainly easiest – to choose one type (or two at a maximum), as both your wallet and your mind will suffer if you try to buy music for, and learn, ten different genres of music at the same time.

The Point: An Audience

It is the most important rule as a DJ always to think of the audience. At the end of the night, the whole point is entertainment – or art, depending on how you see these things. Without an audience, DJing surely becomes something different.

Of course, you have to practise, and you have to practise alone. So when you're ready to practise alone at home, try using your imagination. Picture in your mind three friends that you like and respect for their musical tastes (if this isn't possible then just think of three imaginary people!). Look them up and down to get a clear picture of what they're doing and what

they're wearing. Give them all a drink and a smoke.

Get a good look at the venue – paint it in your mind and hear the music of the guy on before you. It may even help to put up a few posters or pictures around the practice room, showing people like the ones in your imaginary audience. Look at them (smile at the one you fancy) and maybe even throw your fist in the air to get them going. Get in front of your DJ box. Open your record box and pull out three tunes, ready to go live. Hang your headphones around your neck and move up next to the vacant deck.

When you look up over the decks, what do you see? Hundreds of people? Thousands of people? A massive laser show? Imagine what you want to see and try to see it clearly. You have arrived. Now, the job in hand is simple: mix your tunes to entertain the crowd and keep them dancing.

And here's a Golden Rule: you must always play to an audience, not to a brick wall.

Of course, it's also vitally important to see the real, live thing as often as possible, so try to visit venues where you know your kind of music is being played (and don't just hang around the DJ box watching which hand does what – have a boogie yourself). Enjoy the vibe. Get involved with the audience. These are, after all, your people and your (future) audience.

Back To Reality

With the unstoppable rise and rise of DJing, it's no surprise that every electrical outlet wants a piece of the action when it comes to taking cash off the next generation of superstar DJs. Everybody wants to be a DJ, and most people think it's as easy as just buying a couple of decks and setting them up in a flash booth. But mixing records is only part of the job of the DJ; there's also understanding the equipment and doing the homework of finding the tunes.

 DJ Tips

Don't rush out and spend more money than you should on music at this stage – the music will always be there, but your bank may foreclose on your overdraft first thing Monday morning.

Before building a large and expensive music collection, try listening to as many alternative music styles as possible.

Buying records can become intoxicating, almost addictive, so try to exercise some degree of self-control from the outset.

Spending money on new equipment is easy to do, as is spending hours and hours trying to figure it out. The tips you'll get from this book, however, will save you from wasting your money and your time and will seriously improve your results.

A modern top-of-the-range recording studio, with 48-channel mixing desk, twin Macintosh computers running Logic software, plus various keyboards and guitars

The Tunes

During the process of learning to DJ, you'll begin to experience music on a deeper level and you'll learn to appreciate the subtleties of tone, construction and vibe. At any point, this might lead to you changing your alliance from what you, as a non-DJ, considered great, to what you now think of as the perfect genre to perform with.

You have to listen to as many styles as you can, and this is most easily done through clubs, friends and record shops, where you should spend as much time as possible. Libraries also often have a good general sweep of music. And as for the Internet...well, you can search for anything from Angolan throat vocalists to Zambian hip-hop and your browser will return plenty of options. Music content is the absolute must-have for DJs, just as moving pictures are the absolute must-have for a TV station. A DJ without plenty of tunes is like a desert without sand.

Do some homework and locate the local (and distant) shops that stock the widest selection of music. High-street chains will usually sell well-known music more cheaply than specialist shops, but use specialist shops to buy music that hasn't yet reached the masses. Visit as many records shops as you can, and be sure to talk to the staff – they're usually goldmines of information and are often willing to chat. Even dare to ask if they will offer some kind of discount if you buy from them regularly as a DJ. And if you're cool about it, they might even throw a few test pressings your way – you never know!

The Means

Of course, DJing is about tunes, so you'll need to hear them and know them. And, even more importantly, DJing is about the audience, so you'll need to hear them and know them as well. But how do you get there? What's the secret? Practice, practice, practice.

2 SET-UP

'Always acknowledge your audience, smile and be happy – clubbers don't want to watch some anal DJ who never looks up from the decks.' DJ Angel

So, what equipment are you going to need to buy? For every DJ, that's the million-dollar question. And it can certainly feel like you *have* spent a million dollars if you buy all the nice shiny stuff in the high-street DJ store. You may already own some kit, but without one or more of the basic items you're still behind the starting gate. Unfortunately, you'll need to fill in the picture before starting your life as a DJ, even if you opt for only the bare minimum. Remember, though, that even the 'bare minimum' list is frighteningly long...

Turntables
Ideally, the choice has to be at least two Technics 1210 Mark II decks. This is the industry standard and is the model that you're most likely to find in any given club in which you might find yourself gigging. But there are other models that many DJs swear by and even prefer, including the Vestax models PDX-d3, PDX-a1 and the PDT-a2 Scratch deck and PDT-5000. (Alternatively, you could forsake turntables and opt for something flash and modern such as a CD player or even a computer – more on this later.)

Cartridges
Cartridges can cost anything from £40 ($65) to £400 ($650) – sometimes more than the deck itself. The models that are the industry standards are made by Stanton and by Ortofon. You get what you pay for, but for the purposes of practising at home, stick closer to the cheap ones.

Mixer
There are more choices, as far as mixers are concerned, than there are for all the other bits combined. Just be sure that yours has the following:

- at least two channels, although four, five or even six channels is preferable, as it allows scope for a third deck, a CD player, samplers and so on;
- a crossfader, which should be easily removable for regular servicing;
- phono/line switches on every channel (if you're buying a used model, check that these don't crackle or pop when thrown);
- a master volume fader;
- a headphone socket (3/4-inch jack, with separately adjustable volume);
- ground (earthing) point;
- VU meters (these are not strictly necessary but they are useful, and ideally they should be assignable to AFL or PFL levels).

Headphones
Not just any set of household cans will do: they must be durable, be loud enough for club use, have a lead long enough to allow easy movement throughout the booth and be comfortable for long periods, as well as fully enclose the ear. It can be a great experience to use a set of top-of-the-range cans, but do be aware that they tend to wear quickly – many DJs will go through more than three pairs in a year.

Amplifier
When you're practising at home, any hi-fi system will do as long as it's robust enough to handle your style of music. In emergencies, connect the Record Out sockets on the back of the mixer to the Line In sockets on the back of a normal hi-fi. (Be careful, however, as this method often bypasses the master fader on the mixer and the volume sent to the hi-fi may be seriously loud.)

A row of decks at a major club

Slipmats

It needs to be a mat and it needs to slip easily on the platter. Occasionally, in a hot, sweaty club, you'll find that the mat tends to stick to the platter a bit, but you can make it more slippery by putting a bit of plastic underneath it (the inner sleeves of records are perfect – all you need to do is cut them to size and punch a hole through in the middle).

Leads

The cost of all the required leads never fails to shock. Count up all the various leads that you need and see if you can get a bulk deal from your local DIY merchant.

Whatever you decide to buy gear-wise, you must remember that you will require source material (records or CDs), and this will add a considerable further expense. Specialist records are by no means cheap: one vinyl single can easily be the same price as a CD album, so careful consideration must be given to what medium, or source material, you will adopt.

Old Vs New

CD players or turntables? In an actual fight, the turntable wins every time. It's bigger, heavier, carries ultimate respect among users and fans alike and looks cool. However, tip it upside down and drop it from six inches onto its platter and it's busted. The traditional and much-loved turntable does not make a great travel mate due to its delicate tone arm and overbearing weight. So, if you're going to be carrying your equipment to each gig, you should consider this: the source material for turntable mixing is records, and in a fight between a record and a CD, the record wins every time. It is fairly robust and should last forever if it's stored properly (always put a record back in its cover!). CDs, on the other hand, are delicate little puppies that all of a sudden tend to start skipping, jumping and making noises far worse than the worst piece of vinyl has ever done. On the other hand, ask a normal human to choose between carrying 100 CDs up a big hill and 100 12-inch records up a small hill and they will always pick up the cute little pack of silver discs. This is no small matter when planning your domination of the DJing world.

Now enter the new kid on the block: the computer, used as a source player. As a domestic machine for home mixing, your average computer won't last long in this tough wrestling match. A mere few kicks and it will be showing you the familiar old error messages and you know what's coming next: blue screen.

But the PC's source material does win in the big fight (and not just because the other two – the CD and the record – can't actually physically hit it). Source material for a computer is stored as files that don't in themselves physically weigh anything. These files are accessible from the computer's hard drive or the Internet, or maybe from an iPod in your shirt pocket. Mixing music from a computer arguably doesn't look as cool as crouching over a hot deck (unless your audience is the local programming club) and it can sometimes leave the punters thinking you're not actually doing anything aside from clicking a mouse and drinking free beer.

Enter the newer kid on the block: a combination of turntable and computer – 12-inch records that have a special time code on them which controls the music on your laptop computer. Now a DJ can take thousands of tracks to a gig and play them all from vinyl using traditional turntables. It looks cool, it's easy to carry and you get to watch a DVD on it at night in your hotel room. It does, of course, require a pair of turntables and a mixer to work, but these both weigh a lot less than a typical record box.

How To Buy

When you decide it's time to buy some gear, don't buy a thing until you've tried it all – CD mixing, traditional turntable mixing using vinyl records, and digital, computer-based mixing. All have unique qualities and share common ground. For example, computer-based music files such as MP3s can now be played and manipulated using special vinyl on standard turntables (there'll be more on this in Chapter 7).

Where you buy your equipment will depend on where you live. A local specialist retail outlet is always going to be able to offer assistance, and usually the staff will let customers try before they buy. The Internet tends to come in a little cheaper but lacks the facility of letting you try out equipment before you part with any cash. A friend with a set-up is great – especially if they will let you get a spare key cut so you can practise when they're out! But at some point, you'll want to fork out for your own gear – new or second hand, entry level or top of the line.

Used Gear

Excellent gear can be purchased through the small ads, but so can lots of crap. Many beginners will want to start with used gear to get more bang for their hard-earned buck – and that's not a bad thing. Be sure to try out the gear yourself before you let go of your cash. Check that everything moves smoothly (platters spin and sliders glide) and that it's all electrically quiet (no crackling when switches are thrown, buttons hit or sliders slid).

Remember that gear which looks clean might actually be in worse condition than gear which just needs a quick wipe with a rag and some isopropyl alcohol (which evaporates instantly and doesn't harm the electronics).

Also, even if used gear is all your budget can stretch to, there's no reason why you can't still go window shopping. It helps to visit the shiny showrooms and get an idea of what's available and what you like before combing the papers for the same stuff second hand. You'll also get a good idea of what you should expect to pay for any individual pieces of kit, as well as a good idea as to the availability of stuff on the second-hand market overall.

New Gear

Of course, the main advantage of new gear is that you can take it back – and that's a good argument for buying locally instead of travelling great distances for big-city prices. If the savings available in a distant sale are only 20 per cent or less, it's probably worth staying local for that invaluable peace of mind.

Wherever you buy your new gear, if you've got the money then there's no excuse for a rushed purchase:

DJ Seb Fontaine

you've got all the shop assistants within your power, gear prices tend to go up slowly, and sales tend to appear suddenly. A careful shopper who plans meticulously and develops a teased-out relationship with a shop over a relatively long period of time might be able to talk them into cutting a package discount for a full set-up.

The Technology

The basic objective with DJ equipment is to be able to play back music (from a 'source' component such as a CD player or turntable) and have the sound come out of a set of speakers. The DJ needs to have some level of control over the source, the audio volume and the sound that comes out of the speakers.

The way it goes about this, in principle, is not dissimilar to a domestic home stereo. A home stereo has three main components to achieve this end: a source player (for example, a CD, cassette player, tuner or record player), an amplifier, and a couple of speakers. The job of the source player (in this case we'll use a CD player as the example) is to read the disc and transform that information into a low-level audio signal that is sent to the amplifier. The job of the amplifier is to take the source signal (your music from the CD) and boost it in power and volume. The amplifier gives you a variable control to adjust the amount of audio signal it sends to the speakers: the volume control. The final stage is the speakers; their job is to make the source signal audible to the human ear.

The DJ set-up is not dissimilar to the above: it has a source (for example, a CD player), an amplifier and, of course, a pair of speakers. The DJ equipment differs in that there are two source players – for example, two CD players, or two turntables feeding audio to the amplifier. Before that signal reaches the amplifier on a DJ set-up it passes through a device called a *mixer*. The job of the mixer is to give you individual volume control over both source players. This in-line mixer is required in order to balance the individual incoming volumes of the source players before they are sent to the amplifier. The amplifier does the same job as the one in your domestic system, as do the speakers.

The sound that comes out of the speakers can be affected – improved, ideally – through the use of an equaliser box, or *EQ*. You'll be familiar with EQ in a crude form known generically as 'tone control'. Most people first meet EQ when they try to adjust the Treble and Bass knobs on their clock radios. The basic idea is always the same: to set the controls so that the music sounds as good as possible, given a particular set of speakers in a particular room.

EQ comes in dozens of shapes and forms (more on this later), but the most important consideration for a DJ in most clubs is getting permission from On High to change it. Since most DJs won't have read this book, they won't know the first thing about setting up EQ – and club owners know this very well. They know that every DJ they hire will have his own ideas as to how the sound in the club could be somehow 'improved' through some ridiculous (and usually random) personal settings.

Of course, it would be intolerable (and confusing to clubbers) if the sound of a club changed radically every couple of hours, not to mention the damage that would be done to human ears if these lunatics were given the keys to the metaphorical asylum. The result, in 90 per cent of clubs, is that the EQ system will be locked away, out of reach of lowly DJs and usually tantalisingly behind glass doors, apparently with the sole intention of frustrating those DJs who have read this book and so know how to set it properly (and thus improving life for their fans), if only they had the chance.

In the meantime, until you can prove to your boss that you're a careful and safe driver of EQ, you'll have to suffer the indignity of dealing with whatever you're dealt. You'll know that you could seriously improve your set (probably by EQing down the mids and boosting the bass), but you'll just have to grin and bear it.

How It All Works

There's no need for a DJ to be an engineering student. If you know only how to do just what you need to do, and not a smidge more, then you know enough. Time spent learning the extra bits wouldn't be wasted, but it's not required and there's certainly no exam.

As far as turntables are concerned, very few models have more than the required five controls: power, start/stop, speed set, pitch control (or 'varispeed') and

DJ Techniques

tone-arm weight adjustment. The first three are too straightforward to warrant explanation, though it's always worth reminding a person to set the speed correctly (to either 33 or 45rpm). Pitch control simply varies the actual speed of the record by about four per cent (or up to 16 per cent on some models) up or down for both 33rpm and 45rpm, and the centre position is the 'zero' position in which the record should be going at the speed marked on the tin (the intended speed or the speed at which it was recorded). It can be a bit tricky to find the zero position quickly on some models, and if you have any trouble, it may help to mark the zero

Standard connections – how to plug the decks into the mixer

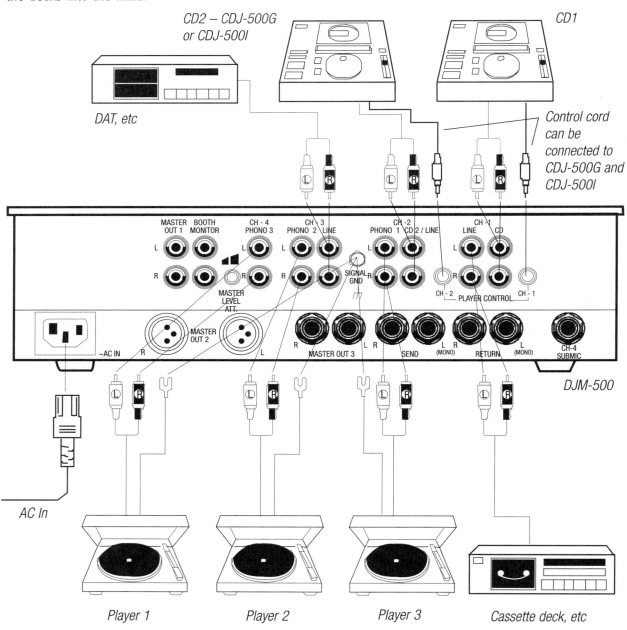

**More connections – how to plug
the amps into the mixer**

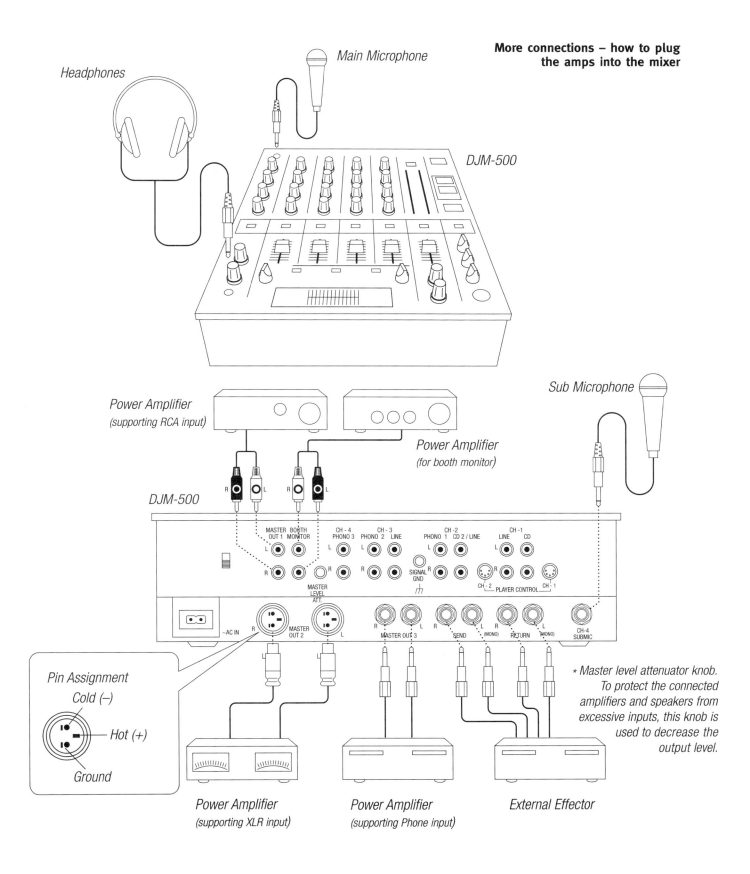

Headphones

Main Microphone

DJM-500

Power Amplifier
(supporting RCA input)

Power Amplifier
(for booth monitor)

Sub Microphone

DJM-500

MASTER BOOTH
OUT 1 MONITOR

CH - 4
PHONO 3

CH - 3
PHONO 2   LINE

CH - 2
PHONO 1   CD 2 / LINE

CH - 1
LINE   CD

L

R

SIGNAL
GND

R

CH - 2   PLAYER CONTROL   CH - 1

MASTER
LEVEL
ATT.

~AC IN

R   MASTER
OUT 2

L

MASTER OUT 3

R   L

SEND

R
(MONO)

RETURN

L
(MONO)

CH-4
SUBMIC

L

L

Pin Assignment

Cold (–)

Hot (+)

Ground

Power Amplifier
(supporting XLR input)

Power Amplifier
(supporting Phone input)

External Effector

* Master level attenuator knob.
To protect the connected
amplifiers and speakers from
excessive inputs, this knob is
used to decrease the
output level.

position (and the other main positions that you might need, such as three per cent up and three per cent down) with a fluorescent pen for high visibility in low light.

It's actually possible to customise your own varispeed, but try this only when you have plenty of time to do it carefully and then to experiment with the result. Begin by removing the platter and, carefully, the protective plastic cover underneath the platter. You'll find a plastic covering with a grille. Remove the plastic screws and take off the plastic covering and underneath there's the speed control, which is a small, blue affair with a circle inside it. Rotate it in a clockwise direction with a screwdriver to increase the percentage of pitch gain.

Tone-arm weight adjustment is a contentious subject. The easy answer is to keep it heavy so as to avoid the inevitable skipping while you're getting busy with your thumb over the spinning platter. The opposite camp preaches against heavy tone-arm weights on the grounds of increasing your vinyl's longevity.

The most hands-on mixing techniques will require more weight on the tone arm than is recommended by the manufacturer, and some extreme techniques require more than can be added using just the built-in weight. On some decks, the tone arm is mounted on a black wheel which has height settings adjustable from 1mm through to 6mm. The higher the arm is raised, the heavier the tone arm becomes.

To adjust the weight of the tone arm, move the small switch on top of the height-adjustment wheel (just beyond the anti-skating dial, if your deck has one) into the 'unlocked' position, then turn the wheel to increase (clockwise) or decrease (anticlockwise) the weight. More weight can be added by moving the cartridge forward. The further forward the cartridge is positioned in the tone-arm head, the heavier the arm will be.

Yet more weight can be added by completely removing the weight at the back end of the tone arm, turning it around and replacing it back to front. This cheeky trick can add up to three extra grams. Of course, as you've known since birth, a massive weight increase of up to three further grams can be added by taping a small coin to the top of the tone-arm head, but this should be reserved for special occasions, as the resulting weight of all the above methods shortens the life of the average record to just under 20 minutes.

For the more daring DJ, there is always the option of reading the manuals that come in the box with your gear. The advantage in doing this is that you have to read it only once and you might figure out whatever quirks your equipment boasts. (The disadvantage is that someone might see you reading it.)

Special Instructions For The Vestax PDX-d3

This model has a 'Quartz Lock' function (to the left of the pitch control) which fixes the deck speed at 33 or 45rpm, but it can also be set at 78rpm by pressing both speed buttons immediately after turning on the power.

The other controls on the left of the pitch control are for putting the deck into 'reverse play' (ie the platter goes backwards) and for turning off the motor – rather than the more familiar method, on the Technics deck, of simply turning the actual power button on and off. There is also a stick-controller which, used like a joystick, fractionally speeds up or slows down the motor. Moving the stick to the left or right radically changes the speed down or up accordingly. Using this stick, you can actually mix without touching the platter, and it's particularly useful when you're playing a record backwards since bizarre things such as reverse direction are seriously confusing to control in the normal way with your hands.

First of all, there are two types of cable that come with a DJ set-up (even though there may appear to be many more): power cables and audio leads. The power cables are the ones that plug into the wall and carry electricity, while the audio leads send (or *buss*) the audio from one device to another.

The audio leads tend to have phono plugs (or 'RCA type' connectors) at each end and normally have red and white tips. The two colours are the visual markers indicating which one goes in the left-hand socket and which one goes in the right-hand socket. These cables do not carry electricity, just audio signals, and cannot harm or shock you if you accidentally touch the bare tips.

To begin setting up the equipment, start with the audio leads and plug the whole lot in, leaving the mains cables to last. The turntables, tape machines, MP3/digital boxes and CD players will each have a pair of audio leads with red and white tips. Remember, these are stereo audio leads which carry two audio signals down the same, dual lead. The left-hand audio feed is the white one and the right-hand audio feed is the red one. These audio leads will need to be plugged into the mixer.

Start with the machine on your left and plug in its audio leads to the mixer. At the back of the mixer you'll find a fairly comprehensive array of sockets for you to choose from: look for the Channel 1 input socket. For turntables, be sure to use the Phono input, and for CD and computer players use the Line input. Plugging into the correct socket is important, although you won't blow either yourself or your equipment up if you get it wrong at this stage. Repeat this routine with the machine placed to your right, only this time look for the Channel 2 audio inputs on the back of the mixer.

Now the mixer will need to be plugged into the amplifier. Again, go to the back of the mixer and look for a pair of sockets marked 'Master Output'. These will be linked using audio leads to the Aux Input on the back of your amplifier. Prior to making that connection, you must check that the amplifier is not plugged in and switched on.

Now you need to run speaker wires – the plain old double-barrelled lengths of wire – from the amplifier to the speakers. On the back of the amplifier you'll see outputs marked 'Speaker Left' and 'Speaker Right'. Using speaker wire, connect these outputs to the corresponding speakers.

Be sure that the audio is connected (the above steps completed) before you power up the mains. Remember to turn the volume on the amplifier down to zero before plugging in the mains. This will help avoid blowing your eardrums out when the system comes to life. The safety rules apply here as with any major electrical power source: don't touch anything with wet hands and don't poke any objects into the mains outlet, apart from properly fitted plugs with the correct fuses installed. It's a good idea to get into the

Budding DJs at Ibiza's Savana VIP Room

habit of always turning on the various power switches in the order of the signal flow: turntables, CD players, tape machines and computers first, then the mixer and any effects and EQ boxes, then, finally – and always last – the amplifier(s).

Keep it in mind that the chain runs from the audio source audio feed to the mixer console audio feed, then to amplifier audio feed and then to speakers. Everything has its own power lead except the speakers, because they're powered by the amplifier. Some speakers actually do have amplifiers built in to the cabinet along with the speaker, and these will require powering from the mains – but this is very rare indeed. All you have to do now is plug your headphones into the mixer. Oh, and learn to be a DJ.

 DJ Tips

Always turn down the amplifier volume control to zero before turning on the power.

Troubleshooting

Most equipment faults fall into three categories: electrical, mechanical or human error. Professional DJ equipment is usually well made, but it can occasionally fail, so have a look at the list of common faults and ways of rectifying them below:

• **Electrical** – Is the switch at the wall turned on? Sadly, this most embarrassing of all mistakes too often rears its ugly head. Once basic stupidity has been ruled out, check the fuses in the wall plugs; if they're all intact, unplug the gear from the wall and check any fuses that may be easily accessible inside your gear. If joy still does not come, ask the owner to check the fuse box that probably lurks in the damp basement of the club. Failing this, if you still can't get the power lights to come on, you'll need a proper electrician.

• **Mechanical** – If a deck won't spin and it's a belt-drive model, it's possible that the belt has come off the drive under the platter. Hold the metal platter a little above the deck and gently stretch the belt around the drive shaft and then around

the gear under the platter. If the tape machine won't spin, make sure that you haven't left an electronic 'pause' button on or that the tape inside hasn't been eaten. (If so, very gently pull the tape out with your hands, an inch at a time, then throw the tape away.) If the CD player won't spin, there's probably nothing you can do (and that's one of the worst things about damn CDs).

• **Human Error** – Unfortunately, human error is usually just forgetting to turn the power on or plugging in a cable. Check the connections again against the instructions above. If you're no expert in wiring up and configuring your system, it might be a good idea to draw a pencil sketch plan of what goes where so that you can slyly check it when no one's looking and maintain appearances of knowing what you're doing.

DJ Tips

If you're not an expert in plugging up and configuring your system, draw a schematic plan of what goes where.

Always carry a few spare 13-amp fuses in case the plug fuses blow.

Other Common Problems

If your deck has this feature, check that it is actually spinning at 33 or 45rpm by reading the red lights and silver dots on the side of the platter. The red light may or may not have an On/Off button or may be controlled by being depressed gently. The middle row of dots should appear stationary under the red light when the pitch control is at zero. If it doesn't, find the position at which the dots stop moving and mark it on the piece of tape that you can stick next to the pitch control at the proper zero position.

As in other walks of life, dirty needles are always a bad idea. They will make the sound fuzzy and can cause the stylus to slide right across the record. Give yours a good blow – with the volume turned down – and be sure not to let any saliva hit it – say it, don't spray it! Check that no grime has built up on the join between

Top DJs at the Ministry Of Sound

the stylus and the cartridge, which can happen even if the stylus is dust-free. Another Golden Rule: if you keep your records clean, you'll always have a clean stylus.

If the sound is coming out of only one speaker, check that the cartridge is mounted securely and screwed in, and that the tiny leads inside it are connected properly and aren't damaged in any way. Alternatively, check that the relevant channel on the mixer is not panned to one side.

If the needle won't stay in the groove, check that the weight on the arm is adequate and that the anti-skating setting is correct. Alternatively, the deck may be sitting on a surface that's not quite level, or there may be fluff on the needle. If you encounter bass feedback (a low-pitched tone), check that the earth leads are connected at the back of the mixer. Alternatively, try lowering the bass EQ setting on the mixer or moving the decks further away from the speakers.

3 BASIC MUSIC AND TECHNIQUES

'The fastest way to get noticed by the press and secure DJ bookings is to produce and release your own tunes.' *Carl Loben, Editor, DJ Magazine*

To be a successful DJ, it isn't necessary to become a formally trained virtuoso musician, but knowing the basics certainly helps.

All music is made up from *notes* (which are pitched high or low) and *beats* (which make up rhythms and are either fast or slow), and DJs are primarily concerned with beats. The rhythms of music are therefore divided into the following:

- **Beats** – The smallest bits, like letters in the alphabet, which we naturally feel in our gut as '1, 2, 3, 4';
- **Bars/Measures** – Like words being made of letters, these are small groupings of beats, usually four in a bar;
- **Phrases** – Like musical sentences, these are groupings of bars (usually four or eight). Phrases tend to have easy-to-recognise endings, much like the drop in a person's voice at the end of a sentence.

Almost all modern dance music has four beats in each bar, and quite often the kick drum (or 'bass' drum) will hit each beat, such as the *boom-boom-boom-boom* kick-drum pattern that signifies house music. The most important rule for identifying beats is that, invariably, a kick drum will hit on the first beat of almost every bar and a snare drum will hit on both the second and the fourth beat of almost every bar. Phrases tend to begin and end with cymbal crashes and other big, exciting sounds that announce the start of new sections – such as a verse, a chorus or a breakdown – and are almost always four, eight or 16 bars long (that's 16, 32 or 64 beats, if you've been keeping track).

It's imperative that you, as a DJ, can identify these elements in any record you ever try to mix. Try to get into the habit of identifying these elements in every record every time you listen to music – they are clearly and equally identifiable in everything from The Carpenters to Massive Attack to Marilyn Manson.

BPM

The speed ('tempo' or 'bpm') of a record is measured by the number of beats that go by in one minute, and it's possible to figure out the bpm of a record simply by counting the beats while looking at a clock. Most dance music – in fact, most music – is identified by its tempo: reggae and hip-hop will usually be at a slowish tempo, ranging from 70–100bpm; house will be at a medium tempo of around 110–130bpm; and techno and drum 'n' bass will have a faster tempo, in the range of 135–160bpm.

The whole concept of mixing two records together is based on the premise that they are at the same tempo, or can be made to play at the same tempo via pitch control. Therefore, it's vital that the DJ feels the tempo of every record intuitively – but then, most people do this, or dancing would otherwise be impossible.

Exceptions To The Rule

There are, of course, plenty of exceptions to these rules, and you will no doubt be frustrated at some point by an exceptional tune throwing up a surprise at the most unexpected moment – but that's the nature of the game. In general, if you're comfortable with these basic musical elements and concepts, you will be well prepared for whatever comes off the grooves.

Cueing And Hand Action

One of the most daunting aspects of DJing for beginners is the task of finding a certain section – or even a certain beat – within the sea of grooves that is a vinyl record. There is a certain 'zen factor' to it, in that most DJs tend to develop a sixth sense for looking at grooves, but there is also a science to it that has some secrets and can be learned.

Begin by staring at a record that you know well. Hold it up to the light and try to perceive the tiny peaks and valleys (use a magnifying glass if necessary). Notice that some sections seem smooth while others appear rough. Notice also that some bits are darker than others.

Hold the record to the light and change the angle until you can clearly see the darker and lighter areas. The darker areas show that the grooves are closer together because the music contains less information and therefore not such a wide groove was required to cut or store that information on the record.

So, with this in mind, if you wish to locate a 'breakdown' on a tune, place the needle in the darker part of the track (and if you need to find the noisiest part of a tune, place the needle on the lightest part).

Note that the darkest bits are the breakdowns

Arms, Wrists, Fingers And Ears

DJing is a very physical art. A DJ needs to develop a symbiosis between his arms, wrists and fingers and the deck and the record on that deck. Introduce yourself to a record by taking an old piece of vinyl that you don't care about and handling it all over. Feel the different textures and get comfortable holding it by its sides (two hands holding each edge) and by its middle (one hand with five fingers cupped closely supporting it with your fingertips). When you're comfortable with the vinyl, get to know the tone arm by softly lifting it with your thumb on the front edge of the cartridge and placing it gently onto the record. Now, with the needle resting on the stationary vinyl, place your middle finger on the vinyl somewhere in the middle of the song, at the halfway point of the grooves.

Get jiggy with it – touch the disc all over

Drop-Mixing

If the music stops at a gig, everyone on the dance floor will look around for something else to do. From the moment you start playing to the moment you end, the music should not stop. You want to produce a constant flow of music for the audience. The mixer is the piece of kit that enables you to keep the music flowing. Your goal when using the mixer is to change between songs without a noticeable clash. To do this, it's important to understand what the fade control on the mixer is doing.

The faders on the mixer console do the job of adjusting the amount of sound that gets sent from the source player to the amplifier; they adjust volume level.

There are two types of fader control. The first is the rotary fader that can be found on very old mixers and a few retro-styled valve mixers; these rotate from left to right to increase the volume. The second type is the more common fader that can be found on 99 per cent of all mixers: the sliding fader. It slides up – away from you – to increase the level of volume. Faders are quite delicate and will wear out after a lot of use, so avoid dropping cigarette ash or liquids into the slot that the fader rides through!

Imagine for a moment that sound is water and the various cables that the sound travels along is piping. Using this school of thought, the mixer controls can now be likened to taps. Pull the fader down and no sound can flow out to the amplifier. It is still being sent by the source player, but the fader in the down, or closed, position stops it travelling on to the amplifier. Push the fader halfway up and half the sound is allowed to travel to the amplifier; open it all the way and you have maximum sound being sent to the amplifier.

So, what will the faders be used for? Your source player – a CD machine, say – has no volume control on it – no tap. Instead, it sends a constant flow through the cable to the mixer. The mixer allows for the amount of flow to be adjusted via the fader, thus regulating a flow of sound that is sent on to the amplifier. The reason why the flow of sound must be regulated so that a constant, even flow of music can be created and delivered to the audience as the DJ switches between songs. The more a fader is opened, the more audio is allowed through and the louder the level of music. By opening a fader quickly, a rush of sound will come out; on the other hand, gently open the fader and a rising

amount of sound comes out. The trick is to manipulate both faders to mould the sounds together.

Tone Control And Smoothness
Even absolute beginners will need to wear out a few brain cells on tone control when drop-mixing. It's often the case that two records, while working together beautifully in tempo and feel, will sound completely different in overall tone and quality of sound. To smooth out such an apparent mismatch, usually only the slightest adjustment is necessary. Try to focus your mind's ear on the 'size' of the sound – is the new record too thin or too bulky in sound compared to the current record? If the new one is too tinny or weak, boost up the bass control a bit. If it's too boomy or plodding, turn down the bass a bit. This is just the most basic of tone control – plenty more comes later – but it's important to begin thinking about the smoothness of your mixes right from the very start.

The DJ Mixing School at Point-Blank's London studios

4 BEAT MIXING

'Always make sure you have sufficient rider as sometimes you will end up spending your full fee.' *Phil Gifford, DJ*

You should now mentally prepare for a journey of discovery – not a particularly long journey, but it won't be a quick trip either. The skill of matching two beats from different tunes together using your turntables, CD players or computer software is a learned skill that will come from much practice. It is important to understand that the learning curve is steep, and at times the task will feel seemingly impossible. If you read and mix – and, when necessary, refer back to this section – then there is absolutely no reason whatsoever why you won't soon master the art of beat mixing.

When young DJs first attempt beat mixing, a look of disbelief tends to cross their faces, and usually, when they hit day 2 it's still there, as they still can't do it. And even as they work so hard, they question why they ever chose to try. Then, all of a sudden, it happens and a smile spreads: they find they're in the mix. So, no giving up, please.

The DJ Skill Set

There are some basic skills involved in beat mixing:

* **Hand And Eye Co-ordination** – You will learn to manipulate vinyl using your hands. At the same time, you will be checking for audio cues or signature sounds on the record. You will use your eyes to position a record ready for beat mixing. All this will happen at roughly the same time, and it will take practice to feel comfortable and at ease carrying out these tasks simultaneously.

* **Assessing Musical Compatibility Between Two Different Tracks** – You will learn to listen to two different pieces of music and compare them. You

will initially be listening to determine if the two pieces of music have any similarities that enable them to work together or complement each other. A funky guitar-led house track will work well with another funky guitar-led house track, but how will it fare with, say, a guitar-led deep-house track? Your assessment will be crucial to the success of your mix.

* **Listening** – You will be listening to two tracks at the same time to determine if one set of drumbeats is going faster or slower than the other. You will be listening to each track in order to determine which set of drums belongs to which track. You will make corrections using the pitch shifter to synchronise both sets of drums, all the time listening to the drum patterns.

Cueing

Now is the time to get intimate with your DJ equipment; time to put into practice most of the lessons you have learned so far. Start by standing behind your decks with the controls facing you. (If you're using CDs or a computer software package, you should find a comfortable position in which to work.) 'Cueing' up a record can be done only manually, using your hand to manipulate the vinyl.

When you're choosing your next tune to play, you need to be able to listen to it without the audience hearing it. This is necessary so that you can be sure that you've selected the correct tune to play, that the speed is correct and that the messy-sounding clatter of synchronisation and alignment during beat mixing isn't heard by the audience. You're able to do this privately by listening through the headphones, and this is called *cueing* (or *pre-fade listening*, because you're listening to the music before it goes out of the channel fader, hence 'pre-fade'). Every mixer has its own arrangement of cue buttons and PFL buttons (a PFL button on any given channel isolates the sound coming through that channel in the headphones), and in most cases the cue button is above the fader for each channel. Have a look in the mixer manual if you can't find the cue or PFL buttons. (No manual? Look on-line. Most manufactures make manuals available for reference over the Internet.)

Set the headphone volume on the mixer console relatively low and set the channel faders to zero – in other words, pull all the faders down towards you. The position of the fader usually has no control over the level of sound in the headphones, so by pulling the faders down you can ensure that no sound will come out of the speakers while you attempt to cue the first track – you don't want your audience to hear you cueing up tracks. Now select the left-hand channel Cue button and play a record on the left-hand deck. If you've selected the Cue button, you should be able to hear the record through your headphones, but it won't be coming out of the speakers.

Once you can hear the music through your headphones, put a record on the right-hand deck, start the record and select the Cue button that enables you to hear it through your headphones. You should be able to hear both records at the same time – although, of course, both tunes playing at the same time will probably sound terrible.

Take some time getting used to selecting the correct Cue switches for each turntable and getting the sound through to your headphones. It's important to keep an eye on the headphone volume level, because in this Cue mode a careless DJ could easily accidentally blast his eardrums with a deafening wall of sound.

Get used to switching from cueing the left-hand track and then cueing the right-hand track – just knowing and feeling instinctively where the Cue switch is. Have a look at the audio levels being produced by each track: ideally they should read the same amount. The mixer console usually has VU meters or a row of LEDs that go from green to red depending on the volume of the music. Are they the same? If not, adjust the gain of one to make them match: use the rotary control above the fader that corresponds to the track whose volume you want to adjust.

Recap

- **Why cue?** So you can monitor the music prior to your audience hearing it.

- **Why would you want to do that?** So you can: make sure the level is correct; select a part of a song without the audience having to listen to you do it; beat-match two tunes together without the audience hearing how you do it.

Hand Action

The next stage is to find the first drum sound on a record. Beat mixing demands that you start the new record – the one you're adding to the mix – at some particularly perfect point chosen by you. Electronic dance music is structured to enable the DJ to beat-mix from one dance record to another, and to help keep things simple for the DJ, the drum beats tend to start at the very beginning of the track – in other words, they will usually be the first thing on the record.

To keep two sets of drumbeats synchronised, you need to manipulate the vinyl on the decks deftly with your hands. Records are manufactured from a delicate material and can easily be damaged by surface contaminants or the acidic properties of human sweat. During beat mixing you will have to touch the grooves, but try to avoid excessive use or manhandling.

Place the record on the left-hand deck and press the Start button so the platter is spinning. There is no need to put the needle on yet, just get the record turning in order to learn a special way of manipulating the vinyl by hand to aid mixing. Before touching the vinyl, you must accomplish a good stance; a position that you're comfortable with. I tend to adopt the stance of a boxer: shoulders back, back straight and right foot forward – only I don't punch people in the face. Then, with my hand flat facing palm down, I bend my elbow and start moving my hand back and forth in a straight line, like a sanding motion. The arm never goes completely straight and the hand never comes back as far as to meet the body.

DJ Techniques

Now place your hand on the record on the left-hand deck and rock the record back and forth.

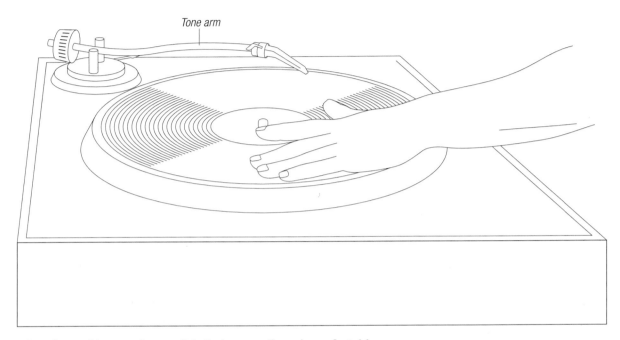

Tone arm

Practise the rocking motion until it feels smooth and comfortable

Get used to the feel of the vinyl under your fingers. Keep your touch as light as possible and avoid pushing down on the vinyl. The goal now is to hold the record stationary while the platter carries on spinning underneath it. Use only the tips of your finger and try to hold gently some part of the record other than the grooved area, such as the centre or the outer edge. Learn how much pressure is required on the vinyl to keep the platter spinning at a constant speed even while the record remains stationary.

Now cue the record up at the start of the song by finding the very first drum beat on that track. Put the needle on the record at the start (the outermost edge). Select the correct speed for the track and press the Start button. You're listening out for the very first drum

beat. Once you've heard the beat, press the Stop button. Pushing down lightly on the label area of the vinyl using your index finger, wind the track back a little. The sound you're hearing is the audio in reverse.

Keep winding the record in reverse gently until the audio stops. You are now just past the beginning of the track. Now wind it forward a little, again using your index finger in the centre of the label, until you hear the very first sound. Is it a drumbeat? If not keep moving it forward until you hear the first drumbeat. When you've found the very first drum sound, lay the palm of your hand flat across the vinyl and rock the record back and forth. If you're too aggressive, the needle will jump from the groove, so practise this until you can roll the record to and fro with the needle staying in the groove. If this seems impossible and the needle keeps jumping, check that you have the turntable tone arm set up properly.

The rocking motion will produce a *chaka-chaka* sound. Take a good look at the centre label of the track and note its position in relation to the tone arm cartridge; this will help you visually to locate the exact start. Rock the record back and forth some more and get comfortable handling the vinyl. When you've mastered finding the first beat of the record on the left-hand deck, do the same on the right-hand deck. Keep working at it until you feel at ease manipulating the records back and forth.

For finding the first beat on CD players, you will need to refer to the manual, and of course the same goes for computer DJing. Each software package has its own way of cueing, however, although most are automated, so this won't be too tough.

Spotting Compatible Tunes

The point of beat mixing is lost if the two records that are to be played together don't work together musically. Some tunes work well together in the mix and some don't. Spotting tunes that will work well together is one of the most important jobs of the DJ.

Let's break the tune down into its basic parts: the drum pattern, the bass line and the melody. Listen to the drum pattern. Each drum kit has its own 'signature' – for example, a drum 'n' bass track will quite often have a rough and raw kick drum. Start listening to the drums (and I don't mean just the drum pattern but the sound of each drum, too). A tune with a loud kick drum and harsh hi-hats may make another tune with a mellow kick drum and breezy hi-hats sound a bit lost when mixed together. The same applies to bass lines.

As for vocals/melody, think Royksopp–Eple. Vocals and melody can really suck your audience in, so play them throughout the set and always be on the lookout for interesting mixes using vocals and melody. If they are familiar, people will sing along with them.

Key, Tempo And Tonality

While different drum patterns will tend to mix with each other as long as the rhythms are similar and run at the same tempo, bass lines and vocals/melody/harmony are a different story altogether. The general rule for this sort of 'harmonic' mixing is that both records must be in either the same key or related keys.

One approach for this would be to study the keys of any records that you intend to mix with, by playing some piano or keyboard over it and remembering which note was the most fundamental or basic starting note for the scale of the key the track is in.

A better approach is to forget all about the rules of music and just get on with it. This sort of trial-and-error approach is by far the best for discovering new and different combinations of records and music genres, but it's important that you do most of your experimentation in the privacy of your own home. Like all the best forms of experimentation, most experiments don't work, and you won't want your audience to suffer the usual fate of lab rats.

While experimenting, remember that it's very rare to find two records that are actually in the same key (considering that you'll be pitch-shifting them up and down willy-nilly in order to change their tempos so they can be beat matched). But just because the keys aren't in fact the same doesn't mean that they won't work together. There is a more subtle version of harmony called *tonality* which suggests that music which, theoretically, should suck, actually can sound fantastic. It's all down to chance, so you've got to play to win.

The main secret is to remember that, even you if try mixing two records of completely different keys or tonalities together and it sounds like a dog's dinner for three minutes, hang about, because you never know when special sections in two tunes will be played together for the first time in history (by you) and sound like God's own white label.

Even a short passage of one minute could be the highlight of your set should you find a magic combination, and most magic moments usually happen when the DJ mixes some old naff vocal over an unlikely bedfellow of a record with a kickin' beat. So, play on...

Light And Dark Music

Aside from tempo and harmony, there is also the issue of vibe. When choosing tunes to beat mix, give some thought to putting like with like (and then like with bizarre to keep things interesting). 'Light' music might be uplifting and high-pitched while 'dark' music might be scary, foreboding and deeply pitched. There's no consensus on the language, but everyone agrees that a bit of planning will help your mixing make sense and 'speak' to the audience. Try to find combinations of musical colour that please you and stick to them. This is the road to art.

Waiting for one record to end and then playing another record is just not good enough for a club environment. True, some people won't care if you can beat mix or not, just as long as the music you're playing is good (and 'good' means that they like it), but if you want to get properly paid for what you play, you have to know how to beat mix. You have to know how to match and blend two songs together so that the music never stops and just keeps on flowing.

Beat mixing ultimately underpins the experience of the partygoer. The listening, drinking and dancing audience gets uninterrupted, continuous music to dance to – a musical journey of songs selected by you, the DJ, that flows and feels natural in pace and tempo. A non-stop musical experience. This constant and even flow enables the dancer to keep a rhythm going, stopping only once in a long while to catch their breath during an instrumental breakdown in the tune.

As a DJ, your job is to maintain a constant flow of music, and in order to do this it's essential that you know how to and can execute a beat mix, that crucial act of being able to synchronise two separate tunes/beats so that they are one. This skill will enable you to make a transition from one tune that's about to end to another tune that's near the beginning without the dancing audience either stopping or noticing any change in pace or tempo.

Once you've mastered the basics of beat mixing, you'll find that it opens up millions of doors to your 'inner DJ' and you'll be able to move your audience musically in any direction you want to take them. Beat

Kiss FM DJ Robin Banks learning to mix at Point-Blank DJ training school

mixing puts you in control, driving the crowd, giving them what they need to keep dancing and enjoying themselves for hours on end. It will enable you to unlock the true potential of your turntables, transforming you from a person with a lot of records and a shiny record box into a proper DJ, or from someone who plays other people's records at a party to the man or woman that makes the party.

The audience will always be looking to you to deliver, to keep them dancing, to keep the party going, to keep the music flowing. Being able to beat mix means being able to keep a dance floor pumping – and a pumping dance floor is a happy dance floor. When you make the dance floor rock, you will be invited back to play again, and with a few offers like that you can start to up your price. Some clubs, particularly house clubs, have seen the number of paying clubbers drop, and they wonder if it's because clubbers are getting bored of hearing 'safe' DJs who mix tunes that...well, mix easily together. This 'safe' mixing is great for making a CD but not exactly inspiring for the audience. So, put the audience first. Play tunes they will like and want to hear, not a selection of tunes that just happen to mix together easily.

What Is Beat Mixing?

When we talk about beat mixing, we are referring to the act of synchronising two or more tunes to create the effect that only one tune is playing.

Imagine you're a passenger on a train. The train is speeding along on a long, straight section of track that runs for hundreds of miles, and about every four seconds the wheels pass over a join in the track. You know it's about four seconds because you're counting the seconds between the wheels passing each join: 'Takady-2-3-4, takady-2-3-4.' The train you're on doesn't speed up or slow down, and you know this because the four-second gap is always the same – never five seconds, never three seconds, only four seconds – between the wheels passing over the joins in the track.

Then, out of the window, a train comes alongside you, heading in the same direction. You listen for the sound of the other train's wheels as they pass over the joins in its rails. Your have to concentrate to separate the sound of each train's wheels, but once

you adjust your ears, you can make out the other train's signature wheel sound quite clearly: 'Takady-2-3, takady-2-3.' The train coming alongside is gently overtaking the train you're on – which makes sense, as the gap between the wheels passing the join is smaller, indicating that the other train must be moving slightly faster. The train you're on is still travelling at its original speed – 'takady-2-3-4, takady-2-3-4' – while the train beside you is still travelling slightly quicker – 'takady-2-3, takady-2-3'.

Out of your window you notice a person sitting in the same seat as you on the other train. This person even looks a little like you and is wearing similar clothes. As your *Doppelgänger* appears to be right beside you, the train he is on is slowing slightly.

The person who looks like you now appears to be stationary: his train must be travelling at exactly the same speed as yours. You check this by timing the signature sound made by the wheels passing over the joins in the track. Sure enough, both sets of wheels are in exact synchronisation: 'Takady-2-3-4, takady-2-3-4.' Should either of the train drivers speed up or slow down by the slightest of margins, the result will be that the two trains will no longer be in perfect synchronisation. Should one train speed up and then slow back down to perfect synchronisation, the result will be that you will no longer be sitting opposite your *Doppelgänger*, but rather opposite a different person on the other train.

With DJing, beat mixing is all about the synchronisation of tunes; both sets of beats on both tracks should be in perfect synchronisation, with neither one going slightly faster or slightly slower. All matching, all synced as one.

Now imagine that you're on that same train but it's pitch black and you can't see anything. You have to use your ears and count to establish if the other train is going faster, slower or at the same speed as the train you're on. All the time, you're listening, counting and re-evaluating the situation; that's what you'll be doing with your two records on the turntables.

Imagine the song that the audience is listening to is the train that you are on. It is running at a constant speed. The new record you want to add to the mix – the record you want to beat mix in – is the train coming up beside you. It's your job as the DJ to manipulate that train coming up beside you, using only your ears and your counting skill, to be in perfect synchronisation with the train you're on (the record the audience is still currently listening to). It's a skill that takes time to learn.

The Pitch Controller

So, beat matching is the act of combining beats from two different records to synchronise with each other, and to make this work you'll need to use the full functions of the turntable. The pitch control, you will remember, performs the act of adjusting the speed at which the record revolves on the turntable platter – move the pitch control up and the record turns more quickly; pitch it down and it slows the platter speed. A DJ needs to be able to adjust the speed at which a tune is playing to align the two tunes' beats together; once he can do it as second nature, he's left free to concentrate on the many other aspects of the job, such as selecting suitable tunes, using the EQ controls and adding effects, to name but a few.

The Beat-Matching Technique

Let's look at a typical beat-mixing problem and solution. In this first case we already know the exact bpms of the songs in question and the DJ simply needs to synchronise them together. Song 1 has a bmp of 120 and the audience is currently dancing to it. The DJ needs to mix in song 2, which has a bpm of 119 and so is a little slower than song 1. To get both songs moving at the same bpm, he will have to speed up song 2.

The reason why he speeds up song 2 rather than slowing down song 1 is that, if he was to slow down song 1 (the one the audience is still dancing to), people would notice a change (and perhaps even stop dancing to see and hear what hell the DJ was doing). Instead, he speeds up song 2 – the one they can't hear – so that the beat mix can be achieved seamlessly and so that, after the switch-over, the music will be continuous in pace.

The DJ speeds up song 2 manually by adjusting the pitch shifter. Song 2 will need to be pitched up (rotated more quickly) just a tad from 119bpm to 120bpm. The

DJ takes a guess at where he'll set the pitch control, pitches it up to that spot and then listens to song 2 to compare its pace with song 1. If they don't run together, he listens to determine which record is now running faster, because he might have made the mistake of pitching up song 2 too much.

If he did pitch up song 2 too much, he makes a second guess at how far down in pitch to try this time, then moves the pitch control to that spot and listens. This is the trial-and-error method that every DJ must use until that magic day arrives when he is instinctively able to predict exactly how far to adjust the pitch control almost every time. When the two are running at exactly the same speed, they are bpm-matched.

Slowing Down A Record

To reduce the speed of a record, place your finger on the outer edge of the turntable, lightly brushing the outer edge of the platter. Only a light application is required. Get used to holding the tune at a constant slower speed for a one-minute duration. Try to maintain a constant speed adjustment – nice and even, so you almost can't detect the record being slowed. You must slow down a record when the beats are coming in too early.

Speeding Up A Record

Place a finger in the centre of the record – somewhere in the label area – and attempt to speed up the track slightly while keeping the new speed fairly constant and even. Pressing your finger down slightly will ensure that the track doesn't slip on the slipmat; the turning action is all in the wrist. It will take time, but the good thing is that you can hear if you're getting it right or not. The goal is to speed up the track, just slightly, and hold it steady without it sounding like it's slurring. You must manually speed up a record when the beats of that tune are coming in late.

Overall Feel

When manually adjusting the speed of a record, you're changing its bpm, and when slowing a record you end up with fewer beats per minute. The amount of speed adjustment required to bring two records into sync varies from tune to tune. Some tunes by chance will require little or no bpm adjustment at all, but of course most will. Practise with as many different tracks as you can to become skilled at pitch shifting.

A good idea to help hone this skill is simply to let a record play and rest your index finger on the label and let it follow the record around, neither speeding it up nor slowing it down. Every now and then, speed it up a bit, let it spin alone, slow it down a bit and leave it running free. This will help you get a feel for the vinyl.

Phrase Alignment

Now that you know how to bpm-match two different records, you need only to 'phrase align' (just like drop mix) them to make a perfect beat mix. Even when two records are running at the same speed, the switch from one to the other will not be smooth if, say, song 1 is playing 1, 2, 3, 4 (a single bar from start to finish) in time to Song 2 playing 2, 3, 4, 1 (two bars, where the first one starts on beat 2 and

must go into a second bar to complete its four beats). Like the train passenger who is sitting opposite his double, the two records must run at the same speed, but they must also be running with synchronised bars and phrases.

So, first you must start by bpm-matching the two tunes, and then you must phrase-align them and make any fine-tuning adjustments to the bpm matching that are usually required (because vinyl records and electric motors are not perfect, and neither are you). Of course, it's possible that your bpm-match will have been so exact that no further adjustment is necessary, and you can then simply drop-mix the tunes together and they'll mix well, but it's usually necessary to make at least some small adjustments.

The trick, then, is to do two things at once: start the deck playing song 2 at the correct place and keep them the two tracks running in phrase alignment all

A top DJ at the Ministry Of Sound

the time while doing the bpm-matching described above to sort out any necessary pitch adjustments.

You might have guessed that the only way to do this is to complete the second task (bpm matching) by making only very small and relatively quick adjustments each time so as not to make song 2 run so quickly or so slowly as to fall out of phrase alignment with song 1. After a few careful trials and errors, small enough to keep the *Doppelgängers* very nearly facing each other, the two records become perfectly synchronised in both speed and phrase, at which point you can fade or switch between them smoothly (and continuously, if desired) without the audience perceiving any difference in speed (so they can easily dance) or in phrase (so they think it might be just one record).

Putting It All Together

Start song 1 playing, put on your headphones and cue up song 2 on the other deck. With the correct cue point selected for song 2, hold the record on the spinning platter at the very first drum beat, ready to release it. Lift one side of your headphones off your ear so you can hear the record the audience is listening to (song 1, on the left-hand deck) through the speakers. Concentrate only on song 1, the record that is playing to the audience; listen to its pace and drum sound. Try tapping your left foot in time to the beat of song 1.

Rock song 2 back and fourth in time to the drum in song 1, creating a *chukka-chukka* sound with the first drum beat of song 2. Now count the beats in song 1 (**1**, 2, 3, 4, **2**, 2, 3, 4 and so on until it gets to **8**, 2, 3, 4). On the 4 of **8**, 2, 3, 4, release song 2. Manually push song 2 forward until the beats match. They may be in sync only for a beat or two, but they need to be matched before you can establish whether or not song 2 is going either too fast or too slow.

Now put the headphones on so they are covering both ears and listen carefully to the pace of song 2. Take off one side of the headphones and ask yourself this question: 'Is song 2 running too fast or too slow?'. You will be able to tell by comparing the two sets of beats. If the beats of song 2 are racing ahead of the beats in song 1, it's running too fast. If, on the other

hand, song 2 is feeling lazy and the beats are coming behind those of song 1, then it will need to be speeded up.

Manually speed up or slow down song 2 until the beats match again. You may need to keep your index finger on the centre of the record and keep winding it to keep it up to speed, or you may need to brush the outer platter with your finger to slow it down a tiny bit in order to keep the two tracks in sync. Once they match, adjust the pitch shifter either plus or minus depending on whether song 2 is running too fast or too slow. Over time, this will become a fluid operation. As you're manually speeding up the track you're trying to bring in to the mix (in this case, song 2), you'll be adjusting the pitch shifter accordingly.

The whole process is made much more difficult if the two records are at different volumes. Use the gain control on the mixer to raise the volume on song 2 until it's slightly louder than song 1, on the left-hand deck. Compare the two for clatter and then gently wind the gain down until both tracks are at a similar level suitable for mixing. Keep manually changing the speed of the record, pushing the beats back into line and adjusting the pitch shifter accordingly.

Before you can bring song 2, on the right-hand deck, into the mix, you will need to carry out a more precise comparison between both tracks. Do this by selecting the cues for both tracks and listening carefully to the kick drum. They should be in perfect sync and sound like only one kick drum. Now wind the gain up and down slightly on song 2, on the right-hand deck, to hear how it sounds up against song 1 at different volume levels. When it feels right, go for it by throwing over the crossfader and listen to your finished beat mix.

In And Out Points

As mentioned above, the moment in the record that you actually choose to throw the crossfader (and thereby open up the beat mix for your audience to hear) is a crucial factor. It's vital that you select a strategic point at which to move from song 1 to song 2. The most common choice – and the easiest spot for smooth-sounding mixing – is the beginning or end of a phrase.

To commit a beat mix at the top of a phrase, it will be necessary to count the bars of the tunes, even while you're already counting the beats of the tunes to be sure that they line up as well. It's not easy, and there's nothing to learn, aside from making sure you remember to count.

The whole process is made easier, of course, if you know your records well. If you're dead sure of when song 1 is about to go into a big stomping chorus, then it's much easier (when you're holding song 2 on a cue-point at the beginning of, say, a breakdown) to start song 2 at exactly the right moment. This can be especially effective if song 1 is a well-known record and, just as the crowd is expecting the big chorus, they get fooled by a surprise breakdown from song 2. As with so much of the art of DJing, it's trial and error and it's practice, but it's also knowing your tunes.

Panning

Panning is the act of moving the sound from one speaker to the other and should not confused with any magazine article denouncing your DJ skills.

The pan control can be found above the channel fader on the mixer console. It's usually a rotary control that, when set to top dead centre, sends an even and balanced audio feed to both left and right feeds of the amplifier. Panning refers to the movement of sound balance between the left and right speakers. For this operation to function, you first need to be using a stereo audio set-up. Most large club venues don't use stereo for the simple reason that the speakers are so far apart that stereo can't be appreciated by an audience. If the vocals were sent to the left speaker and the drums to the right speaker, people on the right of the venue wouldn't hear the vocals, and so for this reason most large clubs are mono – all of the music goes to all of the speakers. Some venues use mono but allow the music to be split between left and right speakers so the DJ can still pan. In most cases, the DJ box is located between the speakers, so panning left and right may sound great to the DJ but the audience may not be able to enjoy the full effect. Look at the venue and ask the

question, 'If I pan, will it just sound like I'm turning the music on and off to people on the edge of the crowd?'

Panning is a great effect on mix CDs and in smaller venues, where the audience can hear the music moving, or *bouncing*, from left to right. By far the most effective place in a tune to use panning is during long sweeps of music that contain no drumbeats or vocals. Breakdowns in tunes sometimes contain strings or other solo notes that have a long sustain, lasting for a few seconds or more while the tune builds slowly back up to the drums. These sustained solo parts can be swept from left to right using the pan control. The effect created can almost make an audience sway with the audio shift between left and right, especially when listening back via headphones. Panning during a breakdown at the same time as introducing a new tune's drum beat to the mix that isn't being panned can create an interesting effect too, as can panning one tune to the left speaker during a mix and panning another to the right speaker.

Experiments are the way to discover how panning works best with your choice of music style and content. If you decide you want to pan during a drum section, try to keep the left-right movement rapid so that no part of the audience is without a drum beat for too long. When panning, always keep in mind the pace and tempo of the music being effected. Try to replicate that as best you can by moving the pan control left and right in time to the tempo of the music.

During drum parts, you should aim to be bouncing from one drum hit to the next. Some mixers have built-in auto-pan facilities that can be assigned to any and or all of the channels. The rate of panning can be varied using the effect-level control. Use pre-fade listen, or cue, to establish the effect that is about to be created first before unleashing it on an unsuspecting audience.

Spectacular effects can be created by setting the panning rate to match the bpm of the tune being played. Fast-building rolling drums that bridge the end of a breakdown can be bounced from left to right to great effect, enhancing the impact of the tune kicking back in full. Try to avoid overdoing panning during a mix, though – probably once or twice an hour is more than enough.

5 TRICKS

'When you arrive at the decks to play a set, check that the crossfader hasn't been turned down by the previous DJ.' Hubert Hudson, DJ and producer

Like a skateboarder, the DJ needs a few tricks that he or she can call his or her own. But luckily, unlike a skateboarder, the DJ doesn't end up with scabby knees when it all goes wrong, and at first it will *all* go wrong. Everyone loves to watch an unfortunate skateboarder make contact with the pavement while going for big air, but no one likes a DJ who crashes a good tune into a wall of sound. That's why it's so important to have an understanding of how to perform tricks and why it's so crucial to practise them in the privacy of your own headphones.

Over the years, hip-hop artists have pushed the turntable to the limit, then they've pushed it some more, and in doing so they've turned what was designed as a device to play back pre-recorded music into a musical instrument in its own right. Tricks are a fantastic addition to basic live mixing because they can bring a set alive and make it special and personal for the audience. Once a DJ has mastered a trick, he can use it to create something unique on the night. It doesn't have to be a complex trick, but it should (in whatever way) add to the music being played.

The style of music that you, the DJ, decide to play will to some degree determine the tricks you perform. For a ludicrous example, you wouldn't expect to hear a wedding DJ scratching hard over Madonna's 'Like A Virgin' (even though it might be a laugh).

Watching other DJs who play the same style (as you tend to do) might reveal a few ideas that you can run home and try out for yourself. For hip-hop DJs, there are numerous 'battle videos' on sale – and the DMC Championships videos are always an eye-opener (check out the dude actually spinning around on a turntable).

Expect your early efforts to sound terrible as you get used to manipulating vinyl on the turntable. A sure-fire way of improving a trick is to record it on tape and then play it back and scrutinise it. Ask yourself this: 'Does what I just did make the tune sound better, or did it sound like someone desperately attempting to show off?' No prizes for guessing the best answer.

Starters For Ten

A simple trick that anyone can get right is simply switching off the power to the motor driving the turntable platter to create a slowing-down effect which can be used as an audio bridge when changing from one genre of music to another. The slowing-down effect works even better when you select a section of the track that has no drum or hi-hat pattern in it – like, say, just a single-string note, which often happens during a breakdown and can last for up to ten seconds. Switching off the motor will cause the note to bend downwards in pitch. Remember to count the beats as if the tune is still playing at its intended speed since, as there are no beats to contend with, you can start the next tune when you count in at the natural phrase point, sounding as if you beat-mixed it perfectly.

Another simple trick is to press the stop button (rather than the power button) on the track you're removing from the mix right at the end of a phrase. Do it on the beat and this will create a fast, sudden slowing down that, if timed just right at the beginning of the next phrase, will make a natural progression. It's also a way of making a transition between tracks that otherwise wouldn't mix.

A DJ can also quickly 'spin back' the playing tune to create a fast rewind effect. Caution needs to be taken here not to wrestle the vinyl too violently or the needle may bounce right out of the groove, creating a new effect – the awful 'jumping needle' effect.

Teaser Drop-ins

By using the hamster switch on the mixer, the DJ can create a drop-in effect. The listener is momentarily afforded a clip of the next track to be played.

Here's how it's done. First, synchronise the two tunes both in bpm and phrase. Check that the levels are the same on the mixer. Then, with the fader open for the next tune to be played and the sound being stopped only by the hamster switch, flick the switch across on a beat so that the incoming tune is perfectly synchronised with the track that's already playing. The DJ is effectively teasing the next track.

This works best if the track that's being teased to the audience has an identifying, familiar signature – for example, a well-known bass line or the identifiable hook of the vocal. The best point at which to perform a drop-in is at the end of a phrase so that the audience will think that the track you're teasing them with is actually about to begin, only to discover that it was a taste of what is to come. Now the audience will be anticipating the arrival of the next tune and readying themselves to dance to it. Get this one right and expect the crowd to roar with delight.

The best tune to tease with is one that's flavour of the month – the big tune that everyone knows you're going to play and have been waiting all week to really let rip and dance to. Once you've teased the track a couple of times and brought the audience to the brink, you can then re-cue it and mix as normal.

DJ Tips

Always be sure that the levels are set the same and the record is perfectly synchronised in both bpm and phrase before applying a hamster-switch move.

Creating Dynamics

The easiest of all tricks to perform – but the hardest to get right – is *dynamics*, or changing the volume. Of course, as mentioned earlier, during the normal course of his set the DJ must always strive to get an even volume from one tune to the next by 'riding' the volume faders: loud records are turned down a bit, soft ones are turned up. Duh!

But there's more. A subtle but effective mood enhancement can be achieved by changing the overall volume of the whole set during key sections. The oldest trick in the book is simply to turn it up, and you better believe it – they all do it. It usually occurs in one of two ways: either by starting the set a bit more quietly than usual by nudging down the master fader and then slowly edging it up until it reaches maximum at the right moment (midnight on New Year's Eve?), or by riding the crowd's own moods by raising and lowering the overall volume just that little bit to correspond with the natural vibes of wildness and chill-out that will occur during any given night in any given club.

Great care must be taken to ensure that the changes are gradual and controlled. This is twice as hard as you might realise because the DJ has to think on two levels: below, keeping the even volume of one record to the next (for smooth mixing); and above, adjusting the overall volume of all the tunes as one. Considering that you'll always be contending with the club's equipment (not your own) and with the club's owner (who cares more about public-nuisance noise levels than anything else), it's much easier said than done. Remember, the goal here – the way to know if you've succeeded with this trick – is to do it without anyone actually noticing, like a magician.

Fills

A very simple but effective trick in the mix is to insert a fill (a drum pattern used in the last bar of a phrase to punctuate the tune, propelling you into the next phrase or section) from one tune into the mix while a different tune is playing. In most records, this will be a short drum roll or a sample of a funky fill, like the one from Roy Ayers' 'Running Away'. The two records must be running at the same tempo for this to work – although, since you're inserting only one bar into the music, this is something you can do to liven things up while you're coaxing the second track to the correct speed.

Choose a track to use as the fill source – one with a brilliant fill, obviously. Beat-match the fill record with the main record that's playing and ensure that the crossfader is fully across to the side of the main tune. Bring the channel fader on the fill tune to the same level as the main tune. Then, on the first beat of the eighth or 16th bar of the phrase (the last bar of a long phrase), bring the crossfader across to bring in the fill from the fill track. Swap back to the main track with the crossfader on the first beat of the next phrase or section of the main tune. The trick can be even more effective if you keep the fill tune's volume slightly lower than the main tune so that the main tune really kicks in after the fill.

Back-To-Back Mixing

This is another very effective trick that you can perform with two copies of the same record. The aim is to beat-match two records but have one record exactly half a beat behind the other record so that you can cut in beats from one over the top of the other to create new and wild drum patterns that are a combination of both records.

To do this trick, beat-match the two copies of the same record but drop-mix one on the half-beat after the first beat of the bar (where the open hi-hat occurs in house music). If you listen to both tracks together on the headphones, you should hear eight kick-drum beats in every bar – evenly spaced – because four kick drums come from each record and they sit half a kick drum apart. Now you can cut in extra kick drums with a swift and sudden move of the crossfader so that the inserted kick drums happen in between the kick drums of the other record, always returning the crossfader for the next kick drum that would happen naturally without the trick. It's vital that you don't lose the main 1-2-3-4 pulse from the first record here, as you would then lose the audience as well.

Generating New Excitement

Excitement can be added to your mix by making live adjustments to the audio. The purpose here is to add some fresh, live audio dynamics to the set. This helps create anticipation within the audience, as they're not sure what's about to happen next. If you deliver the trick correctly, the audience will feel recharged and want to carry on dancing.

It is crucially important that the timing of the trick is carefully considered before execution. For example, you don't want to remove aspects of the audio and slowly reintroduce them back into the mix only to complete this just as the tune goes into a breakdown and all the instruments are out of the mix again, or too near the end of a track so that you end up running out of time. Furthermore, if you remove key aspects of the audio – like, say, the bass line – you'll want to reintroduce them again at the beginning of the next phrase. Ideally, you should build this sort of audio change slowly so that on its completion the trick artificially gives the next phrase in the tune a huge kick.

EQ

Adjusting the level of EQ during a track will create a dramatic effect on the audio. EQ refers to audio equalisation – it can be effectively used to add or subtract 'presence' (or other parts, such as bass or treble) to or from audio.

Most mixers that have on-board EQ adjustment break it down into three parts: treble; mid; and bass. The controls are usually rotary and stacked one on top of the other in a vertical row above the fader (or deck) that they effect. The one at the top – treble – relates to the high end of the audio spectrum, adjusting the high-frequency audio components, such as hi-hats, cymbals and piercing vocals. The mid control adjusts audio in the mid-range of the audio spectrum, such as keyboards, snare drums, pianos and vocals. The bottom control (the one nearest to the user) adjusts the bass audio, or the low frequencies. (Bass is sometimes referred to as 'bottom end', middle as 'mid range' and top as 'top end'.)

The best way to understand EQ is to try to remove the bass from a pumping house track for the last four bars of a phrase and then drop it back in at the start of the next phrase – the audience will respond as if the bass line has just begun again. This removal of a key part of the track builds anticipation in the audience, but it should be used sparingly. The bass can either be dropped back in at the same level it was before it was removed or slowly built back up over four or eight bars to its original level. The same can be done for the top end and mid-range frequencies, but the best place to start when learning EQ tricks is with the bass, as it's integral in driving the audience to dance.

Some mixers come with 'kill' switches installed, which perform the same job as the more traditional rotary EQ buttons but enable you to completely remove virtually an entire range in the audio spectrum at the flick of a switch. They can, of course, be used for effect in the same way as rotaries. For maximum effect try removing the EQ four bars before the end of a phrase and then returning the EQ back to its original position right at the beginning of a phrase and exactly on the beat. As with all tricks, practise this a lot on your own but use it sparingly in a club, as it can become a bit tiring for the audience if over-used. For maximum effect, drop the EQ back into the mix at the beginning of a new phrase and exactly on the beat.

Enhancing The Overall Sound

The shapes of some venue interiors can mean that certain sounds get lost in the structure. Bass sounds gather in corners (and large sofas in the corners of rooms can act as bass traps), and you may find that the music is sounding a little flat and that more bass is required. Adding bass by using the EQ adjustments can restore the missing bass audio.

The same goes for any or all of the audio frequencies. A room with lots of hard surfaces, such as glass, will reflect high frequencies, such as cymbals, hi-hats and piercing vocals. The hard surfaces reflecting the top-end sounds will create the effect of a kitchen full of pots and pans being thrown down the stairs. By removing some of the top-end EQ, the problem may be solved, but if the room really is made of glass then you may have to reposition the speakers to stop so much sound reflection.

When To Use EQ

The moment you should perform EQ tricks will depend on two key factors: the tune and the audience. The tune must have a clear signature sound that, when removed, is very noticeable – usually the bass line. Often the bass line builds as the tune unfolds, and if the DJ can predict when the bass line will make a dramatic change, he can remove the bass line up to eight bars ahead of that point. He then can slowly bring the bass back into the mix over eight bars and hold back just enough bass to give a last push as the tune enters the new phrase with the bass-line variant.

Sometimes the audience will get into the same dance pattern and hardly change for hours due to the DJ's ability to mix smoothly from one similar-sounding tune to another. Adding a little EQ trick can break the routine for the audience and bring them back to a state of awareness. They will be gently reminded that the DJ is busy making the music flow. Try removing one of the frequency ranges from the mix for just the last bar of a phrase and then dropping it back in exactly as the new phrase begins.

When mixing between two tunes, the EQ controls can be adjusted to help make the mix smoother or the EQ can be used to disguise a mix that's going badly wrong. Firstly, let's look at using the EQ to assist mixing two tunes together. By removing one aspect of the frequency range from the tune being introduced to the mix, there will be one less frequency struggling in an already full spectrum. Experiment by removing the bass frequency from the tune you're about to introduce to the mix, then add the tune to the mix and remove some of the top end from the tune that was already playing. Leave both tracks in the mix and listen – you're now creating a new tune using the bass line from one track and the hi-hat structure from the other. When the tracks reach the natural phrase, you can either remove one track from the mix at the same time as returning the EQ switches for the main track to the position they were before you adjusted them, or you can try reversing the bass and top end to create another new track.

Using this technique you can perform long, sweeping mixes that contain no hard jumps or obvious changes in musical structure. Of course, you'll need to choose the right tunes – ie those that already sound not dissimilar and that will give the mix a blending that sounds smooth and flawless.

Secondly, EQ can be used to mask a poorly executed mix. This is an emergency action that must be done instantly upon discovering the fault. In the unlikely event of you finding yourself mixing in a tune that just sounds awful – either because it's wildly inappropriate or because you've cocked up the beat mix or drop mix – the resulting cacophony can be made slightly less deafening with EQ.

The most common clash of music happens as a result of too much sound in either the bass region or the upper-mid region. If you're hearing a muddy rumble from both records together, immediately turn the bass EQ knob all the way down so as to allow a slower and smoother fading out of the outgoing tune. (Remember that, if you simply pull down the fader of the first track, you are surrendering – you're committing the Ultimate DJ Sin by admitting defeat.) Alternatively, if the cacophony if a painful screech of vocals, try EQing them out by turning down the mid-range EQ and then nonchalantly pulling out the outgoing tune. It's a cheap trick, but it often passes unnoticed by the audience.

How To Use EQ Tricks

Timing is everything when performing DJ tricks. Get the timing right and the rest will follow. Here are a few does and don'ts for EQ trickery:

- **Do** listen in your headphones first before attempting to unleash your trick on a paying audience;
- **Do** start and stop the effect at a natural break in the tune – for example, a phrase;
- **Do** return the EQ levels to the zero position before you attempt to mix in the next tune;
- **Don't** yank on the controls, as they will eventually break and fall off;
- **Don't** overuse EQ in a set;
- **Don't** add too much of any one frequency.

By listening via the headphones first, you can get some idea of how the EQ adjustment will sound to the audience, and this is important as adding or removing EQ can dramatically change the character of a tune. Adding too much high frequency, for example, can leave everyone covering their ears (and it won't make you very popular with the promoter for health and safety reasons).

Always follow the natural rhythm of a tune when dropping in effects such as EQ. It's important that you count the beats so that, when the effect is applied, it's at the start of a phrase. This will generate maximum effect from the EQ adjustment.

When you've performed an EQ trick, be sure to reset the switches to the correct (zero) position – the position they were in originally – especially if someone is mixing after you. It's considered rude (insofar as a DJ knows what 'rude' is) not to zero the mixing desk.

It's dead easy to get excited when performing tricks, especially if the crowd is getting off on what you're doing, so you'll need to try extra hard to show restraint when adjusting the controls. The equipment can take only so much pulling and heavy-handed twisting (and nothing kills a set quite like the bass going missing from every second record you play because you snapped off the bass EQ switch during a moment of uncontrollable bass dropping).

Give the music lots of room to do its own thing and use EQ adjustments sparingly. Find a mix that EQing works well for and then use it just once (OK, twice) during the night. (Most clubbers have heard it all before, and overuse of EQ can leave them thinking that they've paid to hear an amateur DJ show off.) This also goes for adding too much of any one particular frequency, as an audience crouching on the floor with covered ears begging you to turn the bass down is not a pretty sight.

Phasing

Phasing might be the most dangerous of all tricks because it is inherently annoying. To properly phasing understand, it's necessary to understand a bit about things called *waveforms*.

All sounds travel through the air as waves, not unlike the waves of water in the sea. They go up and over and they go down and under. In the sea, the undercurrent moves water down and under just in front of the wave that moves the water up and over. If (in some weirdly unnatural world) a water-wave should ever find itself directly on top of an undercurrent, the two would cancel each other out: no wave.

In a sort of 'not very well' way, the analogy does work with wind as well: when a northbound breeze meets a southbound breeze at the same height, you get no breeze – they cancel each other and create a dead calm.

The same is true with music, only it's very unusual for two totally 'opposite' sounds to meet naturally. In fact, the only way to create such an unnatural meeting is to take the exact same sound twice and play it at exactly the same time. Only in music, if the two tunes play simultaneously, you get the same sound but twice as loud, and if they play just one wave cycle apart, you get no sound at all.

The DJ can easily find the 'exact same sound twice' by cueing up two copies of the same record at the same time. But what exactly is 'one wave cycle apart'? Well, suffice to say for now that it's pretty damn close. In fact, because we are imperfect humans (well, some of us, anyway), we only need to try to play the two records at exactly the same time and, as hard as we might try, we'll always fail by at least as much as 'one wave cycle apart'.

So, to begin your adventures with phasing, cue up the same tune on both decks and try as hard as possible to play them exactly in sync. If the volumes and the EQ are also equal (or as near as dammit), you'll hear the sound of LSD (or, at least, the way makers of 1960s movies thought LSD would sound).

Once you've managed to achieve this basic psychedelic sound, try experimenting with slight changes in speed on one of the two discs, either with the pitch or a slight thumb-touch to slow one down. Any slight change in speed on either deck, or a slight change in volume or EQ, should send the phase effect into orbit, aurally speaking.

Phasing is often found as an electronic effect on various effect boxes, but, while these do work very well, there's nothing to compare with the raw and extreme sounds that can be achieved through the use of two copies of a record and a thumb.

A Cappella Mixing

An a cappella is the vocal of a tune minus all instrumentation. It is recorded as if the instrumentation exists and can be played back over a similar-tempo track.

An a cappella can be used in several ways: it can be brought into a studio and added to new instrumentation, such as drums and bass line, to create an entirely different record from the original; alternatively, the a cappella can be used as a filler over a different tune. For example, if the a cappella in question is a known song with a particularly well-loved hook, you can use the hook over another song when

DJ Tips

The secret of making a live a cappella mix sound great is to find a well-known vocal and lay it over a well-known instrumental.

there is no vocal. This can be done using scratching or as a simple drop. (Be careful, however: it almost never works to play two vocals over each other, causing them instead to clash and crash.)

Another use (and a killer one) for an a cappella is to take the instrumental of a much-loved tune and mix an a cappella of a completely different tune over the top of it, creating an entirely new mix of the records. This is a trick that has made the names of many Superstar DJs (Sasha, to name but one). It may take years of searching to find the right a cappella and the right instrumental, but once you do, it could become a signature tune and make your name.

Remembering Keys, Tempos And Vibes

The first decision when planning an a cappella mix is whether the instrumental and the a cappella are in the same (or in a roughly compatible) key. If they are not, the whole darn thing will sound just plain wrong.

The next major decision is the tempo: the relative speeds of the two tracks. Speeding up an a cappella too much on a normal turntable will cause the vocal to sound as if it's coming from the mouth of a cartoon character, so ideally you want the instrumental and the vocal to be at nearly the same bpm.

Probably the best a cappella to produce in a live show is a lyric from an old track which is played against the instrumental of a new track or, alternatively, the a cappella of a brand new track played against a well-known older instrumental. A good remix will get a crowd going wild and give you something exclusive with which to tower over other DJs.

To get the two tracks to blend nicely, you may need to use a little EQ, but try to avoid adding too much top end to the a cappella as it tends to make things a little ear-splitting. If your nerves get the better of you, consider recording the mix at home onto a CD; that way you can play it into the mix on the night without trying to pitch-shift both tracks together at the same time as being offered another drink and being chatted up.

Tonality And Tempo Problems

If you've got an idea for an a cappella record and an instrumental that seem to work together in all ways but one, there may be a solution...

If the problem with the match is one of tempo – ie one record falls behind or speeds ahead of the other to such a degree that the pitch control on both decks won't cure the problem – one possible solution would be to use the pitch control on one deck twice. This nifty trick is done by recording the tune onto a CD with the pitch control at maximum and then playing it back with the CD's own pitch control adjusted as needed. All CD machines that are designed for DJ use have a pitch-shift control (some have a master tempo control, which will keep the tune in key at the same time as the tempo is increased). Done properly, a well-executed a cappella/instrumental combo can't be beaten; it's the jewel in the crown of a great set.

If the problem is tonality – ie the keys or pitches of the two tunes seem wrong – you could try renting or borrowing a harmoniser from a friend (they're too expensive to buy for just one tune). A harmoniser can actually change the key of a tune without changing its tempo. In this way, you can try different keys or pitches over the other record without affecting the tempo or groove.

Practical Considerations For A Cappella Mixing

Many a cappellas are placed as the last track on a 12-inch single and are usually recorded at the same bpm as the main track on the record. When you're adding an a cappella to an instrumental, you should tap your foot along to it to give you a feel of the beats and to help you lock it in with the instrumental. Then, once you have it locked in bpm, you'll need to cue and start the a cappella at the end of the phrase of the instrumental track that's already playing. The two tracks will be required to run together in sync for quite some time, so you'll need to adjust things slightly in order to resynchronise both tracks. Avoid manually speeding

up or slowing down the a cappella during vocal parts, as this is quite obvious to the audience due to the change in vocal pitch and tone; instead, manually adjust the speed of the instrumental until both tunes are back in sync or push the a cappella track into place during the silent moments in the track between lyrics.

When practising a cappella mixing at home, it's worth taking notes of which tunes work well together. You can write a reminder on the sleeve that indicates which a cappella works with the instrumental and by how much it will need pitch-shifting either up or down. Of course, this will be only a reference, but it will save crucial time and brain capacity when you're playing live and have other things to concentrate on.

Effects Units

There are many types of effects unit available on the market now. Some are designed for and dedicated to DJ use and others are intended for studio use (or even guitar use) but can easily be plugged into a standard DJ mixer. By far the most convenient effects unit is one that's built into the mixer. It will require no wiring up and comes with selector switches that enable the DJ to route the effect through any desired channel. However, remember that, if you practise on a mixer equipped with effects, there's no guarantee that the venue you play at will have the same mixer.

Taking your own mixer to a gig can be a pain, as you'll need to unplug the source players and the master audio-output cables plus the mains power lead, not to mention get the approval of the club owner/engineer. The same can be said for all effects units, but if you're determined, go for it – if nothing else, adding some effects will certainly make your set different from what the other DJs are doing.

Ambient Effects

Most effects units – and even some mixers – have reverb effects. While some refer to it as 'echo', it isn't and it shouldn't be confused as such. Strictly speaking, reverberation is the sound of a large room – that is, the sound of the music decaying away after the original source sound, while an echo is a distinct repeat of the original sound, as when you yell into a canyon: 'Canyon...canyon...canyon...canyon...'

Reverb is an unusual effect to use in a club, because most clubs are big rooms that have their own natural reverb, but big reverbs can be effective in a set if used dramatically and, as always, sparingly. The biggest reverbs on electronic effects units will use the terms 'large room' or 'large plate' in the name and will have decay times of three seconds or above. Be sure to try each setting out beforehand, and listen to how it sounds on the floor. The most effective use might be to turn on the reverb for very short periods, such as for just one word in the song, especially – although it's a bit obvious – the last word of a verse or chorus leading into a breakdown.

Delay Effects

Delay effects – or 'echo', as above – are the workhorses of dance-record producers. Reggae – not to mention every other kind of music – would be nothing without them. Every effects box and most mixers have some sort of delay feature.

In short, the idea is to repeat a certain sound – a word of vocal or perhaps a drum beat – in time with the tempo. Not only does this add a bit of excitement but it actually adds to the groove, so it's crucial that the timing of the delay is synchronised with the speed of the tune. As a rule of thumb, remember that a record at 120bpm will love a delay of 500ms (milliseconds) or multiples thereof, such as 1,000ms or 1,500ms. If the tempo is slightly faster than 120bpm, the delay is slightly shorter than 500ms. If the tempo is slower, the delay is longer.

The other main concept here is feedback. (Not the kind that wails and deafens you, mind.) When used in this context, the word *feedback* refers to the knob on the delay box that recycles the repeated delay into itself, thereby giving you several repeats of the same sound. So, instead of getting just one repeat (a 'slapback' echo), you get ever-decreasing repeats ('echo...echo... echo...echo...').

There's no way to accurately describe a good use of delay effects, but trial-and-error practice with a good record and a delay box is about the most fun a person can have. By setting aside several hours and getting lost in the headphones, any fool is bound to strike it lucky with a good effect before it's over.

Samplers

Samplers are a way of storing audio that can be manually triggered to play back through a mixer. Until just a few years ago, owning a sampler was a luxury left for the most expensive music studios, but with the crash in the price of computer components (namely memory chips) samplers are now cheaper than decks. The amount of audio that a sampler can store and replay depends purely on the size of its memory. The more audio you want to store, the more memory it must use.

Most studio samplers can be triggered in two ways: either via the Play button on the front panel of the machine or via a keyboard connected to it via a protocol (computer language) called MIDI. For the DJ, samples can be triggered using a piano-style keyboard, with the pitch of the sample changing depending on which key is pressed on the keyboard. Alternatively, the sampler can be set up to play different samples, or sounds, for each key on the keyboard.

DJ Tips

A home-recorded CD filled with your own samples is a cost-effective way of making your live set more personal.

Purpose-built DJ samplers now exist and are fully portable and easy to use. They mainly offer the function of sampling parts of a track in a loop form and enabling the DJ to fire the loop back in at any point during in his set. This affords the DJ the opportunity to extend and remix tunes on the fly. They're great tools if used correctly, as the DJ can sample the parts of a tune that the audience enjoys the most and add them back into the mix later in the show.

If you just want to play jingles or pre-recorded audio clips in your set, burning the clips to a CD is a good option. It's much cheaper than buying a sampler, and most clubs have at least one CD player that offers good cue and pitch-adjustment controls. Alternatively, a MiniDisc recorder can be used. These usually offer more than adequate cueing and playback functions and are fully portable. Most MiniDisc players have a record facility to record up to an hour's worth of samples on one disc.

Pre-recorded Sounds

When recording audio for use as a sample, it's important to achieve maximum (or, at least, adequate) audio quality from start to finish. To do this, you need good source material to begin with.

For example, let's say DJ Earth Mover wants a friend who has a good voice to say his name a few times so he can play it at the beginning of his set. He plans on playing the sample back live in the mix using a CD player. He will record and edit the vocal sample on his home computer. It's important that a good-quality microphone is used and it is connected to a quality soundcard on the computer. A quiet room with reasonable acoustics will be required (with no passing traffic and some furnishings to help eliminate room reverb and extraneous noise). The person doing the voice-over must be about four inches away from the microphone and should be aware that words with a strong 'P' will create popping sounds as the breath rushes into the microphone. (If the vocal required has any Ps in it, try turning slightly away from the microphone as the Ps are pronounced – this will prevent the breath from going directly into the microphone head.)

Let whoever is doing the voice-over listen to an example of the music it will be played over. This will give them an idea of the pace and energy levels they need to deliver for the piece. A 'drop' or voice-over for a chill-out session should be laid-back, whereas a voice-over for a full-force drum 'n' bass DJ would want to be harder in delivery.

The record levels must be set on the device – in this case, a computer. Use the visual level meters to get a good signal: the signal should be hot, but not over-peaking in the high red. If the levels are too high, the audio may distort and some of the words will sound chopped. If the level is too low, the audio will need boosting later, and this may bring background hiss into the equation. Try to get the person doing the voice-over to keep a steady volume throughout the reading. Record several takes of the voice-over in one go so you can choose the best one from a selection.

Once the vocal has been recorded, it will need editing. ('Editing' here means removing any sounds that appear just before, or just after, the vocal drop

and aren't required.) The voice may sound a little cold on its own, so try adding just a little reverb or delay to add warmth to the vocal. EQ can also be added to boost any part of the voice that lacks punch.

Every audio-editing package is slightly different in operation, but most computer packages use these same principles. The audio is stored on the hard drive and is shown on-screen as a waveform with peaks and troughs, representing the changing volume of the audio. A thin line will represent quiet, or silent, areas. Most editing packages sample in stereo, so the peaks going up will represent one channel and the peaks going down, the other. The audio is recorded from left to right; moving a cursor into position will enable the user to make a cut in the audio. The cut, or edit, is 'non-destructive', so if it's wrong, the Undo feature will return the audio to its original state, as before the edit.

The recorded audio on the hard drive doesn't change; the software just logs a number of 'in' and 'out' points. This means you can chop the audio and experiment with different edits without destroying the original recording. If the voice-over performer said the word 'DJ' exactly how you wanted it to sound on one take and 'Earth Mover' on another, the two individual parts could be edited together to create the complete piece, as if it had been one continuous take.

Many computer software editing packages are available on-line for free. They're quick to install and, once you've grasped the operational aspects of the software, they're fairly easy to use. However, they're capable of performing some powerful tasks. Try copy-pasting the word 'Mover' on the voice-over and spacing it evenly along the track to create a loop of the word. (Now the voice-over will go something like this: 'DJ Earth Mover Mover Mover Mover'.) You can add volume envelopes to a word so that it fades away over time.

Once you're happy with your sample, save it, burn it to CD (and label the CD clearly so you can read it in a dimly lit club) and add it to your record bag.

DJ Tips

Record vocals in a quite room with the windows closed to avoid recording the sound of passing traffic or other unwanted sounds.

Beat Juggling

Beat juggling is the act of making a new drum pattern from two records by playing them slightly out of synchronisation. To practise performing this trick, you must use two copies of the same record. Ideally the records will contain very little instrumentation or lyrical content so that you can clearly hear each beat of the tune as it's playing.

Set the two tracks to run at the same speed and then start the track on the left-hand deck ('deck X'). Open the fader for deck X so that you can hear the music through the speakers. Now cue up the other track on deck Y and, on the phrase, start it playing. Using the headphones and PFL switches in the normal way, sync the two tunes together. When they're synced manually, very slightly touch the outer rim of the platter of deck Y, thus slowing it slightly. The beats of both X and Y should now be off-beat. Thus you've offset the beat on deck Y just enough for it to sound like each kick drum from song Y is exactly halfway between each kick drum from song X.

Next, make sure the hamster switch is all the way over to the tune that's playing out – in this case, deck X, left-hand fader. Push up the fader for deck Y and, on the beat, throw the hamster switch. The effect created should be the sound of an extra beat as you throw the hamster switch back and forth. This effect works especially well with hip-hop and can be expanded to include physically moving the track back one beat as it's playing out and then throwing the hamster switch over to the other deck, where the tune is still in its original sync.

If this is performed correctly, the audience will listen intently, swaying their heads back and forth and pausing in time to the juggling beats. It's quite a tough one to master, however, and takes great rhythmical timing. With practice, though, beat juggling can be executed at a live gig and command huge respect from the crowd.

DJ Sasha

6 SCRATCHING

'DJing is very much like making love to a beautiful woman: you cue it up, drop it in and then try your hardest to keep going without it falling out.' *Simon A Morrison,* DJ Magazine *columnist*

Pray silence, for in the beginning, there was nothing. God said, 'Let there be recorded sound,' and Thomas Edison created the 'sound-writing machine'. Then, RCA used a flat-talking disc to record music for the masses, and it was good. During times of battle, the flat-disc player was used as a tool to entertain overseas troops; those that operated the spinning-disc machine came to be called DJs – or disc jockeys – and some were good.

The year is 1969 and DJ Kool Herc develops a hand-on-vinyl manipulation called 'cutting breaks'. Using two identical records he mixes percussion by switching from one turntable to the other. Hip-hop is born, and its birth is immaculate. The 1960s end and so, as night follows day, the '70s begin, and then there is Technics, and it is good. Grandmaster Flash releases a flat-disc recording called 'The Adventures Of Grandmaster Flash On The Wheels Of Steel'. A new sound is born, and it is very good. Towards the close of the '70s, Technics carries out improvements on the motor and gives us the SL-1200 Mark II. It is so good that the design still exists today.

Scratching is the art and science of manipulating a sound by hand using a record to supply the audio and a crossfader to edit it. The DJ, for example, takes just one sound from a whole song and manipulates it in such a way that it becomes a rhythm in its own right. The DJ is editing – or lifting out – a chosen sample or piece of audio content from a song and repeating it a number of times by allowing the sample to pass the needle and then physically pulling the record back into position and repeating the process. From the audience's perspective, they get a one-off, unique musical experience that has been created live.

Scratching was first adopted by the hip-hop fraternity. The music they play is at a slower bpm than, say, house, and it has plenty of space to enhance the audio content by adding vocal stabs and other scratching techniques. The DJ can select from a range of samples and repeat them during the set, thus giving the set a sense of consistency. A scratch doesn't have to be complicated to gain respect from the audience, and overkill can be a real turn-off (unless you have the skills of one of the top-ten scratch DJs in the world).

It's amazing just how little scratching is required to really bring a set to life, making it special to the crowd. And, of course, scratching isn't exclusive to hip-hop DJs; nearly everybody seems to do a little bit at least once in a while. A scratch DJ with rhythm will make a dance floor really move; good rhythm comes from lots of practising dancing in time to music.

Equipment, Hardware And Records

To start scratching, you need only a pair of turntables (or, at a push, CD players) and a slipmat. For turntable scratching, a slipmat is integral to all aspects of scratching, as the DJ must be able to slip the record back to the desired position quickly. Keep the slipmats dry, and if they get damp – perhaps due to the sweat from the crowd – change them for fresh ones.

🎧 DJ Tips

If your slipmats stop slipping, you can take a plastic bag and cut out the shape of the slipmat from one side of it and place it between the platter and the slipmat.

The turntable must have a good, stable tone arm, as this is the part of the deck that must keep the needle in the groove under battle conditions. It should be weighted rather heavily (and, ideally, according to the operation manual, though this isn't a law).

For best results, the turntable must be a direct-drive model, as belt-driven turntables take longer to reach the correct speed due to the energy from the motor being displaced through a rubber band. Turntables that are direct-drive (meaning that the motor itself is driving the platter without any form of energy transfer or middle piece), on the other hand, get up to speed almost instantly. Time is of the essence when it comes to scratching as everything happens so quickly.

Perhaps the biggest problem in learning to scratch is keeping the needle in the groove. As the platter is moved back and forth violently, the needle can be easily jogged from its resting place. Also, the working surface must be stable – you'll have no joy scratching if the decks are wobbling when you handle them.

 DJ Tips

If your deck is dead stable but the needle still won't stay in the groove, try a heavier needle that's sturdy enough for scratching.

The mixer will also get a full work-out when you're scratching, so choose one that's robust and has a hamster switch (crossfader). All faders should have a fast, smooth action and have enough space around them for you to operate them without accidentally knocking another switch.

 DJ Tips

Spend time gently working your moves and applying more vigour later, once you've mastered keeping the needle in the groove.

Battle records are great for scratching. They offer a fairly comprehensive mix of samples and beats on one piece of vinyl and can usually be found in hip-hop music shops. Yes, that's right, just ask for 'Battle Weapons'. Trust me.

The Moves

Some years ago, when hip-hop DJs turned the record player into a musical instrument by handling the vinyl roughly as it rotated on the platter and manipulating the audio output levels using the faders, DJs started taking their skills more seriously. Those requisite skills include beat counting and accurate timing with a lot of sophisticated ear-hand-eye co-ordination. So it must be understood that a methodical and patient approach is necessary if you want to achieve some level of success.

When you scratch a record, you're running a sound (or a 'sample') back and forth under the needle so that each time you push the track forwards (clockwise) you hear the sound play, and each time you pull the record backwards (anti-clockwise) you hear the same sound playing backwards. By pushing or pulling the record faster, you make the sound higher-pitched, and by moving it slower, you make it lower-pitched. Performed rhythmically, this is – in its most basic form – the familiar *wukka-wukka* (or, more accurately, *chukka-chukka*) scratch – known to DJs as the 'Baby Scratch'.

Body position is important when scratching: you don't want to be all cramped up in a corner with no space to move in. The scratching DJ needs to be able to jump, or hop, between decks and mixer. (Hip-hop actually originated from DJs who hopped between tracks to keep the music flowing.)

Careful attention must be given to the hand-on-vinyl position: it should feel natural. Start by laying the hand flat or horizontal on the record, as shown in the illustration overleaf. Let your arm follow the line created by the flat of your hand. The desired position is one of hand and lower arm (to the elbow) being completely level and horizontal. Move your body left and right until the position is most comfortable. Now raise the hand, leaving the tips of your fingers on the vinyl with the lower arm following the angle of accent. Reposition the body for maximum comfort and space to work. Rock the hand back and forth, pushing and pulling the vinyl; look at your hand and arm to assess what's moving. Try rocking the track back and forth from the elbow so the body is static but the lower arm and hand are moving.

Now gently introduce more of your body to the motion. The more you move to the rhythm, the better the rhythm that can be achieved. Use plenty of body

Start by laying your hand flat on the vinyl

movement but not so much that it impairs the hand-on-vinyl movement.

When you have body movement and control over the hand-on-vinyl to the degree that the needle is staying in the groove, it's time to look down at the position of your feet. If you're scratching with your right hand, you should have your right foot forward, your left foot a shoulder's length away and back slightly to the left and your right knee slightly bent to allow movement to be absorbed through your legs.

Good posture is vital, but you should also feel comfortable

Moving up the body, your hips should be at a 45º angle to the front edge of the deck. With your back straight but leaning forward, re-adjust your feet to make all this comfortable. The stance now adopted will enable the rhythm to pass freely from the ear to the brain and on through the whole body, delivering precisely timed and synchronised movements to the hand manipulating the vinyl. Your spare hand will be used to control the faders, and the favourite among these for scratching is the hamster switch.

Imagine that a track is playing on deck X to an audience and the DJ has a track on deck Y that is cued to a kick drum. With the up/down faders open for both decks, the open audio output is now controllable only by the hamster switch: it cuts the audio from left to right as you throw it. The sideways movement of the switch will allow for audio 'stabs' to be played. The switch is being used to 'edit' the audio in a live, real-time environment. The wrist of the hand operating the hamster switch is crucial to your control over your speed and timing in manipulating the switch, so position yourself far enough away so as to avoid knocking any equipment or other switches on either the deck or the mixer.

Putting It All Together

The DJ uses a combination of eye, hand and ear co-ordination to achieve the end result of a rhythmic scratch. The eyes are used to 'spot' a part of the track that is to be repeated, and by far the easiest way to re-spot a track after playing a sample from it is by using the centre label as a visual reference point to assist in returning the track to the position it was in prior to the scratch move. If the centre label is white – and has sufficient empty space on it in between any writing already on it – then the DJ can mark a pointer on it, which makes it easy to spot the very first place that the sound they wish to sample passes the needle.

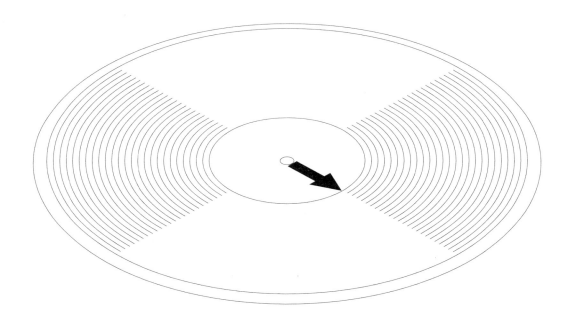

A reference marker helps when re-spotting a track

Every time that same sample is played, the DJ can use the arrow as a visual cue to return the track to the start position. Some centre record labels are easy to work with, as they have lots of straight lines that will line up either to the needle or to some other fixed point on the turntable. But, of course, it doesn't matter

what fixed point you use to realign the track (it could be the pop-up light or the power on/off switch); as long as it's a fixed point to which you return, the record will be in the correct position.

If the centre label is covered in circular graphics and there is no natural co-ordination with any fixed points on the deck, then you can use a small sticky label to mark the point at which the sample sound passes the needle. This can be stuck in the space on the record at the end of the tune or in that gap with the sweeping, gapped grooves near the outer edge of the centre label.

If you're planning on scratching live in a club, it could be worth considering using glow-in-the-dark labels to mark crucial positions, while another technique is to place an angled piece of tape right next to the groove that has the desired sample – because of the angle, the needle will be guided to the cue point.

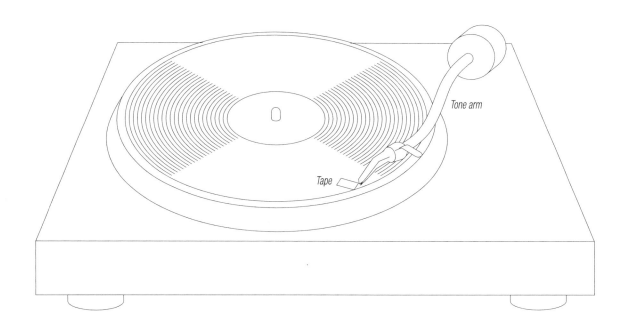

Tone arm

Tape

Use tape to help line up a sample

Using a visual or physical cue on the track to enable the DJ to re-spot the beginning of the sample means that the headphones can be removed, and with the headphones out of the equation, the DJ is free to listen to the master audio output through the monitor speakers. This ensures that the scratching you hear is the same scratching that the audience hears.

The hand co-ordination in scratching requires great dexterity when handling the spinning vinyl. Only the tiniest movement of the record passing under the needle is required to create a scratch sound, and your hands will need to be able to move quickly and accurately to re-spot the track properly in the original position. The speed at which you push the record past the needle will have an enormous effect on the sound generated, so take time to practise and familiarise yourself with how much pressure and speed you need to apply in order to get the record to move back and forth under the needle.

A Practical Example

Place a record on deck Y, put the needle at the start of the track and let it begin. As soon as you hear the first beat, stop the record from turning by physically pressing your left index finger against the outer edge of the platter, thus forcing it to stop completely.

Using your right index finger (placed in the space between the end of the music on the record and the label), gently rotate the track backwards until the very first beat is heard. Leave the left finger in position, to prevent the platter from rotating, and then reposition your right hand. Your hand should be nearly flat, with only the tips of the fingers making contact with the surface of the vinyl.

Use your index finger to stop the record from spinning

Release the left index finger that was restricting the platter from rotating, allowing it to turn freely under the stationary vinyl. It's important that the platter is spinning freely under the record, as the platter takes a moment to get up to speed when it's started from the stop position.

Listen to the effect and try again. Put the needle halfway into a tune that's stationary on the platter. Open the fader and press Start. The audio on the record speeds up as the platter approaches working speed. (If the platter is being slowed or stopped by the down pressure applied by the DJ's hand on the vinyl, when you release it there will be a slight delay as the record gets up to speed.) Timing is critical – these potential danger areas that could throw the timing out must be eliminated.

Get comfortable with holding the vinyl stationary while the platter spins underneath it. When you finally do feel comfortable with the motion of rocking the first kick drum back and forth past the needle, you will know that you're ready to scratch. In fact, you're already scratching, albeit in the most basic form. To help you follow the learning curve (and to prevent boredom from setting in), swap and change the master track that you play in the background, but try to swap the track for one that's at the same bpm.

You'll also need some sample parts. Start with a kick drum – as it can easily be found – and later try to add vocal stabs. Start by listening to as many vocal samples as you can handle. Choose just three that you really like and use them. As you progress with your scratch, begin to add more vocal drops.

Basic Scratches
Baby Scratch
With the fader open, find the first kick drum and rock the record back and forth about a fingernail's length. It will make two distinctive sounds: the first is the kick drum and the second is the kick drum playing in reverse as you pull the record back to the start position. The sound made is usually called a 'chukka' sound as in 'cha' (the sound made by the kick drum when the record is going forward) and the 'ka' sound emitted when the record is being pulled back to the start position.

The Baby Scratch is essentially just the moves discussed above, although now it will be delivered along to the beat of another track (preferably at a low bpm while you're learning). The Baby Scratch is the audio of the sample going forward and backward past the stylus, delivered in time to music (slowly at first, then built up to speed).

Count aloud, repeating, '1, 2, 3, 4, 1, 2, 3, 4.' On the 3, push the record forward and hold it, making sure the platter is spinning at full speed under the vinyl at all times. Count '1, 2, 3', and on the 4 pull it back to the start position. Use your ears to judge if the timing is good.

When you've this mastered, play a tune on the other turntable. Count or clap along to the tune to ensure that you're selecting the correct timing point. Rhythmically push and pull the track in time to the beat. This will have the effect of the extra kick drum fattening out the overall sound. (It may help to move your body to the rhythm of the playing track in order to ensure that the same rhythm being supplied by the playing record is demonstrated in the scratch.) The speed at which the track is pushed forward and pulled back over the kick-drum sound will affect the overall sound: faster moves give the audio a higher pitch, slower moves give it a lower pitch. When practising this move, you should be attempting to maintain a rhythmic motion throughout your body.

Forward Scratch
For the Forward Scratch, the DJ must both manipulate the vinyl by hand and operate the hamster switch. The hamster switch will chop, or edit, the audio being fed to the audience. Applying the fader at the correct moment will enable the DJ to edit out unwanted parts of the sound: for example, you might want to use the sound of the kick drum going forward – 'cha' – but not hear the sound of it being moved back to the start position – 'ka'. To do this, the DJ will use the hamster switch to 'kill' the audio when the record is travelling in reverse.

Imagine that deck D has a record playing out on it and you're going to use deck Y to scratch from. Find the kick-drum sample on deck Y and cue it up. With both faders open, the hamster switch should be fully to the left, allowing audio only from deck X to be heard by the audience. Count along to the track playing on deck X, slide the hamster to the middle position and – on a beat – push the vinyl on deck X forward so that the 'cha' is heard. Now slide the hamster switch back to the left so that only audio from deck X can be heard by the audience. Open the hamster switch to allow audio from both channels. Scratch on the beat and then slide the hamster switch back to the left. Pull back the vinyl to the start position and repeat.

Once you've mastered this skill using a kick drum, try using a spoken-word sample. Practise playing in the sample at an even speed so that the word being spoken is clearly audible and maintains a constant speed even when repeated. Use the EQ controls to enhance the sample so that it's well defined.

When you're comfortable with words, scratch the spoken-word sample over another tune and, by closing the hamster switch off before pulling the record back to the start position, the audience won't hear the word in reverse. Timing is of the essence.

Practise by recording a few minutes of yourself forward-scratching with a spoken-word sample over another tune. When you're listening back, identify areas where the timing isn't tight and practise keeping a better rhythm. Listen for how well the scratch can be heard: is it too loud? Too quiet? Too much bass? A little screechy?

Backward Scratch

The Forward Scratch move is basically this: hamster switch open; forward scratch; hamster switch closed; return record to start position; repeat. Now, keep the hamster-switch movements the same, only this time open the fader when the record is being pulled back to the start position and – easy as that – you've done the Backward Scratch.

Scribble

This is really just the Baby Scratch with a twist. Get the Baby Scratch going with a 'silence, sample, silence' arrangement. Now tense the forearm and let it shake quickly but with a minimum of movement. No hamster-switch operation is required here, but arm speed is the key, so practise making that arm freak out.

Chop

Before attempting the Chop, your technique with the hamster switch must become swift. Get used to sliding it quickly to the right and left by flicking it using the index finger and thumb. Do this in time to the music. The effect you should be creating is one of the forward sample playing out of the speakers and the reverse sample not playing out of the speakers. Start to master the move, as with all other scratch techniques, by doing it in slow motion. Always make sure your eyes are watching the needle alignment so that the record can be re-spotted. Your ears should always be listening to the timing of the sample being played and its balance in the mix. Your hands should always be relaxed, agile and busy.

A Chop Scratch is what the name implies: the DJ 'chops' part of the audio out, using the hamster switch, to edit the Forward Scratch so that only a part of it is played.

Say, for example, your vocal sample was the word 'beautiful'. By opening the hamster switch for the 'beaut' part of the word and then closing it before the audience hears 'iful' the DJ can chop down the length of the sample and create an edited stab. It can be used effectively to tease a forthcoming track.

To perform the Chop, you'll need to get a sample rocking back and forth over another beat. Look closely to ensure that the record being used for scratching is being pulled back into the correct start position. On the forward stroke, quickly stab the hamster switch on and off, thus chopping the word. Use the finger and thumb to flick the hamster switch and add some wrist action to speed up the movement. Try it at slow speed to start with and gently increase the bpm as you improve.

Advanced Scratches
Chirp

You'll know you've got the Chirp Scratch licked when all the birds outside your window are calling back to you. The secret lies in maintaining synergy between the hand pushing the record forward and the other hand opening the hamster switch at the same time.

Start with the sample cued and ready to play and with the hamster switch open. Push the record forward to play the sample and at the same time cut off the hamster switch. As the record is returned to the start of the sample, turn the hamster switch on. The sound at the end of the sample should be nipped off using the hamster switch to perform the edit. Try to make it sound as clean (and bird-like) as possible.

Tear

The goal of the Tear Scratch is to create three individual sounds from one sample. This is done by dividing the sample up using pauses in the movement of the record past the needle. This is, of course, demanding on the hand that is physically controlling the record. The trick of a Tear Scratch is to move the record back and forth

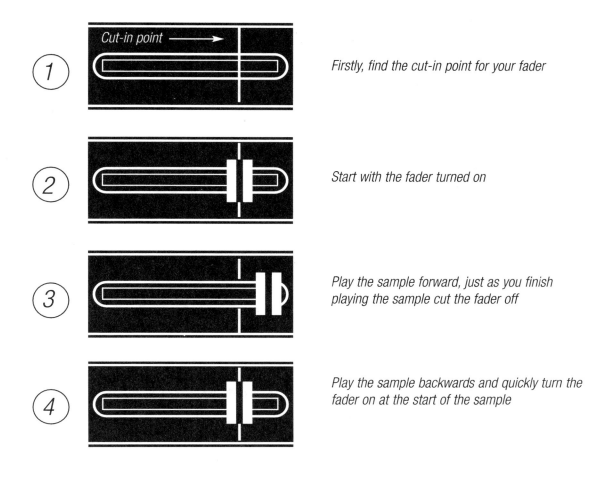

1 — Firstly, find the cut-in point for your fader

2 — Start with the fader turned on

3 — Play the sample forward, just as you finish playing the sample cut the fader off

4 — Play the sample backwards and quickly turn the fader on at the start of the sample

5 — Keep repeating this process over and over: sample forward; cut off at end; sample backwards; cut on at start. Keep practising until you get an even 'chirping' sound and hand movement.

The Chirp was created by Jazzy Jeff and is a popular scratch which is still used by many DJs

in a rhythmic motion, so start by pushing the record forward through the sample, pause, come back halfway through the sample, pause, and then drag it back the rest of the way to the start position. This move is the 'forward-back-back' move: one stroke forward and two back. The combination of Tears can be changed to bring about new effects within the scratch.

Transform

With the Transform, the DJ creates a series of chops on a sample, so a very long sample will be useful here – for example, a long, moaning 'arhhh'. Push the record forward to play the sample and, as the record moves, use the hamster switch to switch the audio off and on quickly. The DJ should be making a cut-up version of the original sample. Now, to make the Transformer really stand out, try switching the hamster fader off and on during half beats. The goal is to make the sample bring an essence of funk to the table.

Crab

Crabbing is a way of achieving four sounds from one sample. It's relatively easy to understand how crabbing works, but it's a tough cookie to master.

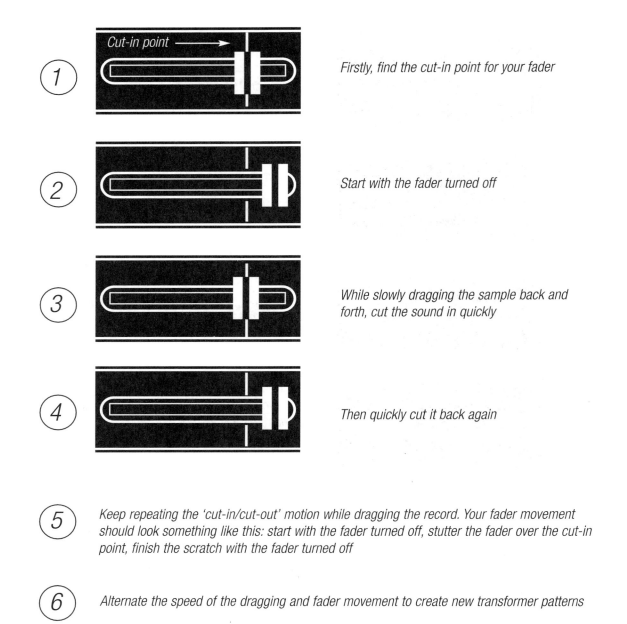

1. Firstly, find the cut-in point for your fader

2. Start with the fader turned off

3. While slowly dragging the sample back and forth, cut the sound in quickly

4. Then quickly cut it back again

5. Keep repeating the 'cut-in/cut-out' motion while dragging the record. Your fader movement should look something like this: start with the fader turned off, stutter the fader over the cut-in point, finish the scratch with the fader turned off

6. Alternate the speed of the dragging and fader movement to create new transformer patterns

The Transformer was revolutionised by DJ Cash Money's famous patterns performed in his DMC routine

The sequences of events that take place are as follows: first, get the record ready to scratch by moving it back and forth so that your chosen sample is playing in a rhythmic fashion. Now turn your attention to the hamster-switch hand and prepare to perform a manoeuvre that, inevitably at first, will go horribly wrong. But that's OK, because here are some helpful techniques to master the move you are about to attempt.

First place your thumb and little finger on the hamster switch and click the little finger so that the ring finger is on the hamster switch. Then, with finger and thumb on the hamster switch, click your fingers again so that your middle finger takes its place. Finally, click one more time so that the index finger joins the thumb on the hamster switch. What a racket!

The desired operation will use the thumb to return the hamster switch to the off position; the clicking of fingers momentarily puts the hamster switch in the on position. Snap your fingers at speed as the sample passes the needle. When mastered, it will create four very distinct sounds.

Turntablist DJ Q-Bert created the Crab, which is considered by many to be the fastest scratch in the universe

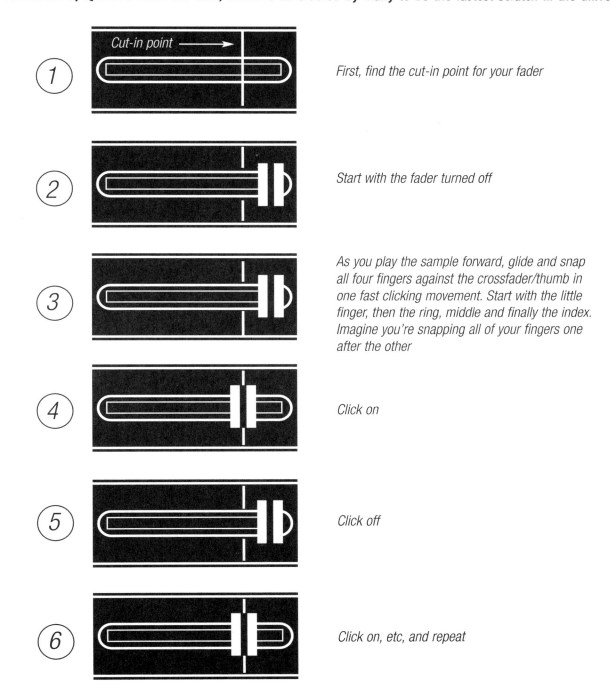

1. First, find the cut-in point for your fader

2. Start with the fader turned off

3. As you play the sample forward, glide and snap all four fingers against the crossfader/thumb in one fast clicking movement. Start with the little finger, then the ring, middle and finally the index. Imagine you're snapping all of your fingers one after the other

4. Click on

5. Click off

6. Click on, etc, and repeat

To perform the Crab technique successfully in the fullness of time, start by practising the flicking motion, but practise one finger at a time. If you're deadly serious about it, carry a spare hamster switch with you and practise the movement of clicking all the fingers against the thumb.

Flare

A one-click Flare will create two sounds each time the record is moving either forwards or backwards. A two-click Flare will create four sounds in each direction. The technique for both is the same, only the two-click Flare happens twice as fast.

This is how the Flare is achieved: with the hamster switch open, push the record forward, cut the sound off using the hamster switch and then immediately switch it back on. Now bring the record back to the starting point and, as you do so, cut the sound off and then back on again. (Hand speed is important, so it's best to play in that sample nice and slowly to get warmed up.)

To help with the rapid hamster-switch movement required, try pinching the switch rather than swiping it from side to side. Pinch it quickly like it's something hot and practise this pinch technique so that it momentarily clicks the hamster switch off and back on in one pinch movement. The thumb hits the hamster switch and turns it off; the finger turns it back on again straight away.

Orbit

The Orbit is essentially a two-click Flare. First, find the cut point for your crossfader. Start with the fader turned on and, as you drag the sample forward, quickly 'click' the fader off. Immediately click it back on to the cut-in point and click it off again, and finish with the fader turned on. As you drag the sample backwards, quickly click the fader once again.

Hydroplane

This is an interesting and uncommon technique. The Hydroplane is performed by gliding your finger (or fingers) along the vinyl surface against the record's direction of rotation. The end product is a gritty, bassy sound that makes the sound vibrate.

Tones

This technique is fascinating to watch performed. The Tones effect is the creation of a melody from the most boring of sounds: tones (such as the test tone used by many broadcast stations for the Emergency Broadcast System test, so somehow you'll need to find a record containing a constant tone or noise for at least one minute). The DJ simply plays the track, using the pitch control and RPM switch to vary the pitch to create 'melody notes' and incorporates scratching at the same time to create 'notes' of varying lengths. All this is done over a track on the other deck and, if the pitching matches well, it creates a wild, musical effect.

Beat Juggling (Or 'Looping')

The act of juggling beats enables the DJ to extend a part of a tune such as, for example, a four-bar loop, and with the loop extended, he could add scratches on top. The solid, consistent loop will help focus the attention on the added scratching.

Two identical records are required. Find an instrumental bar in one track and find the same in the other. Play one bar from one deck and then play the same bar from the other deck. Use the hamster switch to make the audio cut from one record to the other. Keep repeating the process and you have a loop – the same bit of a tune extended for as long as the DJ desires.

The secret to looping successfully, however, lies in the edit. The start edit point should be the first kick drum in a bar. Use the visual cue on the record centre to realign it quickly and count how many times the record has rotated so that it can be spun back efficiently every time. Keeping the loop tight is a definite must, so consider, at first, using an eight-bar loop, as this will give you more time to re-spot the track back at the start.

When the art of looping is mastered, try reducing the length of time between edits – all the way down to just 'one beat/one edit' (and also try running the beats slightly out of sync to create a new beat). Now add some of the scratches already mentioned (at least, those that you've mastered so far) to the loop by using the record cued to play next.

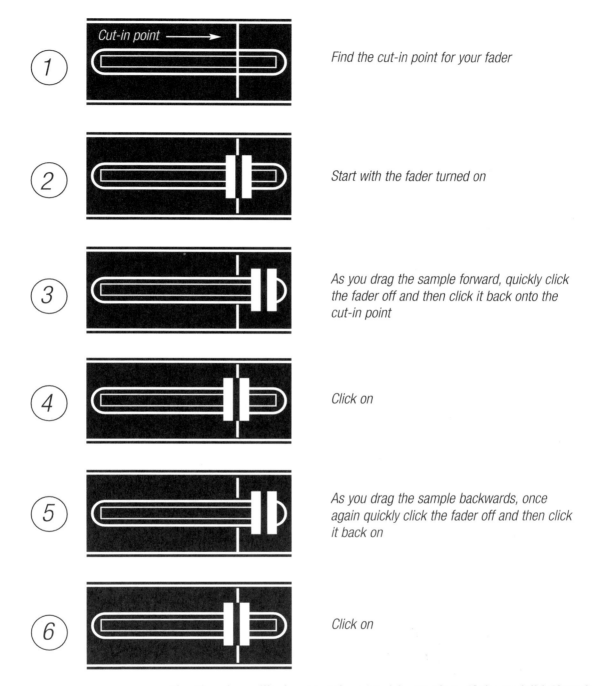

1 Find the cut-in point for your fader

2 Start with the fader turned on

3 As you drag the sample forward, quickly click the fader off and then click it back onto the cut-in point

4 Click on

5 As you drag the sample backwards, once again quickly click the fader off and then click it back on

6 Click on

The Flare is an illusion scratch created by DJ Flare of the Invisibl Skratch Piklz

The Strobe

And finally, a scratch-like effect for the house DJs called the Vornstrobe. Listen to a house track (in which the 4/4 beat goes 1, 2, 3, 4, 1, 2, 3, 4) but imagine it in your head as half time, with the beats happening only half as often (as in '1, 3, 1, 3').

The trick is to get two tracks in the mix and to stop one of the tracks for each beat. The track will be physically stopped between each kick drum and each beat between the kick drum. It requires virtual mixing in the head before going for it live, and after four, eight or even 16 stops the record can be released to continue playing in the mix.

Try to pat the record with the tips of your fingers to get it to stop. It is, of course, essential that the slipmat is allowing the platter to continue spinning and that the turntable has a suitable amount of torque to keep things moving.

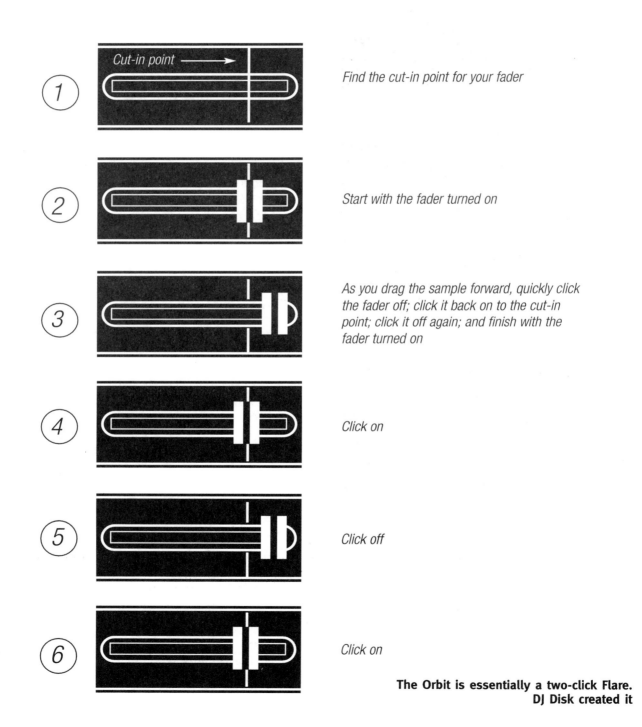

1   *Find the cut-in point for your fader*

2   *Start with the fader turned on*

3   *As you drag the sample forward, quickly click the fader off; click it back on to the cut-in point; click it off again; and finish with the fader turned on*

4   *Click on*

5   *Click off*

6   *Click on*

**The Orbit is essentially a two-click Flare.
DJ Disk created it**

Back-To-Back Mixing

Combine two DJ kits together and two DJs can scratch at the same time to the same tune; or one person can build, say, a drumbeat with a just a kick-drum sample and the other person can scratch over that.

The equipment set-up works like this: connect your system as you would normally and then plug the record output into a spare line input of the other mixer. Hey presto, now all four decks can be operated at once.

This can be a complicated and confusing operation for the first few minutes, but stick with it. There's no actual 'trick' here, just a strange combination that gets you thinking and experimenting.

Three-Deck Mixing

With a constant flow of DJs working the controls harder and harder as the night goes on, club equipment can end up taking a real pounding. To ensure that a night doesn't come to an early close due to deck failure, some club owners add an extra deck to the equation. But, of course, DJs don't see it as an emergency tool – they turn it into just one more weapon in their arsenal to jump all over and make good use of.

To set up your own three-deck system, you'll need a mixer with at least three phono inputs and three decks. Set the system up as normal then add the extra deck either on the left- or right-hand side, depending on your handedness and whatever you fancy.

The additional deck can be used in several ways: to drop an a cappella into the mix at the same time as beat-mixing other tunes, to scratch a sample, or even to mix three music tracks at once.

For the three-tracks-at-once technique to work in a live situation, serious consideration must be given to the selection of the tracks. Two busy tracks being mixed together will require at least some EQ to take away any resulting cacophony, but add a third busy track and very quickly it all tends to go very wrong.

Tracks that have lots of space to breathe during them are best for three-deck mixing, and it's definitely worth marking those tracks that have minimal instrumentation and could easily benefit from another track being played at the same time. The minimal track can be cued on the third deck and dropped into the main mix to create a theme throughout the mix.

And To Get Really Good…

They say that, if you want to get good at a game, play against someone who's better at it than you, and back-to-back mixing is no different. 'Playing against' another DJ will improve your skills and is great for sharing scratch ideas as well as learning new actions and tricks. Competitiveness makes you work harder, and being able to step back and watch someone else scratch can help no end when learning techniques. See and hear and mix with a friend – or ten – whenever you can and see where it takes you.

7 DIGITAL MIXING

'What separates the wannabes from the players are that the pros have the latest beats, they do more than just beat mix, and they know their records properly.' *Paul Thomas, DJ and producer*

If the words *digital mixing* conjure up images of banks of hi-tech equipment being operated by a geek with spots the size of his last pizza in a room with no windows, then it's time to think again. Digital mixing has now come of age and is about to boom in every direction, from CD mixing to computer mixing.

The word *digital* refers to a storage technique: the music is stored as a binary code (a series of ones and zeros) that can be read back by a device that in turn reproduces that information as music. Because a computer is already working in binary code, it's only logical that music can be stored on a computer's hard drive and then be manipulated by various kinds of software to enact DJ mixing.

This progression has happened in the last ten years as computers have moved on from being huge calculators that possessed the audio qualities of a doorbell to becoming complete music-solution tools. Thanks to fast chipsets and superior programs, a high-street-bought computer is now well up to the job of producing music and mixing it live.

The thing is, however, the computer or CD deck as a DJ tool is only ever as good as its operator. No machine can – or will ever – replace the DJ as a performer who selects the order of music and uses his or her skills to manipulate tunes together to keep a dance floor bouncing.

CD Mixing

First out of the bag in the line-up for digital mixing is the compact disc, as tried and tested in houses around the world and, more recently, in clubs. For international DJs, a solution was required to overcome the problem of transporting large quantities of pre-recorded music.

Vinyl has a serious weight problem: 200 records is about as much as any one person would ever be willing to carry at a time. With CDs, on the other hand, you can burn 15 tracks on to one compact disc (and carrying 20 CDs cannot be considered hard lifting for the weakest of us), and hey presto! You have 300 tracks easily to hand.

Also, for the international DJ, he can carry these tracks as hand luggage, thereby removing the temptation for baggage handlers to 'borrow' a DJ's set. There was a point a few years ago when DJs were checking in their records at the airline desk and seriously wondering if they would ever see them again. Life's worst nightmare is to arrive in a country in time for an event only to find you have no music. One can hardly pop to the local record store and replace it all.

So, from the start, the CD seemed a good solution to the DJ's problems, though early CD machines offered not much more than pitch shifting and stop and start facilities. More recently, however, the machines have learned to loop, edit and even cue-play two tracks from the same disc, thanks to a built-in buffer memory.

Using a CD machine is fairly simple: the track is cued via a large wheel on the top of the device to wind the disc forward physically until you find the first beat. Pressing the Cue button marks a cue point that can easily be returned to by pressing the button again. Pre-fader listening is done in the usual way, via headphones through the mixer desk. Pitch shifting is also adjusted in the normal way, but what does differ is that, instead of speeding up or slowing down the vinyl by hand, you use the wheel on the top. A little nudge is all that is required to pitch the tune into sync.

The wheel can also be used for scratching. Denon first built a pro CD machine with a larger-than-normal wheel on the top that actually spins, thus giving the sensation of a record going around. Vinyl DJs found it easier (and always will) to synchronise tracks using the spinning wheel as opposed to the static wheel.

But don't be fooled: CDs are by no means the same as vinyl. (Try fanning yourself to keep cool in a steaming night club with a CD.) Apart from their lack of cooling ability, CDs are prone to damage and a misplaced fingerprint can cause the laser which reads the digital bits on the disc to jump or get stuck in a nasty clicking loop.

Great care needs to be taken when handling and transporting compact discs. When the disc is not in the player, it should always be kept in a cover, and by far the easiest method of keeping CDs from getting damaged at a gig is to use a CD wallet. These can be flipped through like a book, allowing you to see your discs quickly and clearly. Some CDs have very little information printed on the actual disc, so a special pen – found in most computer shops – can be used to over-mark the CDs so that they can be located easily, even in low light.

One feature found on some CD players – and which can be used effectively in a set – is the Master Tempo button. This will enable the DJ to change the pitch of a track without changing the key of the music. Often, when the DJ pitches up a track too much, the vocal tends to sound odd and fake. With the Master Tempo button, the CD player samples the track and plays it back at the same key, only faster.

The Master Tempo button can also be used to take old classic tracks that are so often just too slow to mix over modern dance-music tracks and enable the DJ to remix it over modern dance records – the two tracks can be blended as one without the obvious sound of the vocal having been speeded up. (Househeads should go and get a copy of John Paul Young's 'Love Is In The Air' and have a go. This track can now be pitch-shifted from its original tempo of around 119bpm up to and faster than 126bpm without any problems, with the vocals sounding as though the song is being sung by his lesser-known little sister, Joan Pauline Younger.)

Connections

Connecting a CD player to a mixing desk is not dissimilar to connecting a standard turntable. The CD player has the same two main cables: the power cable, which goes straight to the power outlet on the wall, and a pair of stereo phono leads, which go to the mixer. These stereo leads will have a red and white phono plug at the end of the cable. The appropriate colour phono plug should be connected to the line input on the back of the mixer (and the Phono/Line switch that relates to that line input used for the CD player will need to be selected to Line). Adjust the gain for the selected channel to a low setting if you're switching between Phono and Line as a CD can be much louder than a piece of vinyl.

Cueing/Playing

Each machine will have its own unique quirks, but basically they all have a Cue button and a Play button. The point of the Cue button is to find a spot in a song and be able to mark it so that, at the press of a button, you can quickly return again to that exact same spot. This is useful for finding the first beat of a phrase on a dance track for mixing.

To find and mark a cue point, start by pressing Play and listening to the opening of the track. When you hear a potential cue point – for example, the first drum beat – then press the Cue button. The chances are that you won't hit the button exactly at the point that the first drum beat starts, so use the jog wheel on the top to find the actual start of the first drum beat. When you think you have it, press the Cue button again. To test if the right point has been selected, press the Play button and listen. The drum should kick straight in without any delay. Take note that, if at any point the Cue button is pressed again, the CD player will remember that new cue point of the track.

Looping

Looping refers to repeating a section of music over and over. The section should roll naturally over the edit (or the point where the piece of music starts again). To achieve this, a suitable 'in point' and 'out point' will need to be found. (The first beat of a new phrase is a good place to start.) Now you have the choice of how long you want the loop to last: one beat, one bar, a whole phrase, whatever. Most CD machines offer the choice of selecting loop length merely by pressing a button.

Here's a good place to start experimenting with different length loops: the loop should sound natural as it passes the edit point or the 'in-out' point. No stuttering or sudden key changes should occur.

Using Loops

Loops can be used in several ways. One use is to extend a piece of music while the DJ ensures the next track will mix smoothly into it. Another use of a loop is to sample a hook or part of a tune which can then be 'played in' over and over again on top of another tune. This works well if the loop being sampled has a well-known hook in it.

Short one- or two-beat loops are most effective if they're fired in just as a tune is coming out of a breakdown and is about to drop. The DJ can artificially hold back or sustain the drop, and this will help build anticipation on the dance floor.

CD Sampling

Using the CD player as a sampler will enable any DJ to make his or her set unique and personal for the night. A fistful of samples and loops on a couple of CDs can send a crowd wild. (Some of the best samples are available from the Battle Weapons range. These usually come as vinyl and are used by the hip-hop crew for scratching.) You can also sample a bit of a great tune that everyone loves – for example, the opening bass line to a Michael Jackson or James Brown number – and play it back as a loop over an instrumental.

Stabs

Stabs are short pieces of vocal and/or sound effects (often referred to as SFX). They can be played in over a track to bring extra life to an otherwise dull spot in a tune, and they can also be used as a signature for a DJ. If the DJ's name, for example, is DJ Shotgun, a sound effect of a shotgun could be dropped into the mix every so often to make the (overstated) point of announcing who's on the decks.

A sweeping sound effect could be used to bridge between two songs to create a soundscape; this is particularly useful for chillout songs or where two tracks just will not mix (for example, when you're changing music genres).

Whatever you're after, always try to find sounds that complement the music. Sound effects and stabs that mimic the music in some way are the best. A hard, violent stab sound against a smooth jazz number can leave the audience baffled as to what the DJ is trying to achieve musically.

Autostart

Most CD players come with an autostart feature, but in order for it to work the mixer must be of the same brand as the CD player. The autostart feature can be used on the crossfader to perform the technique more easily and to exchange samples from CD players. The idea is the same as the use of the autostart feature on the crossfader when executing a drop mix, except that here we don't want the whole track but rather just the selected sample.

Check that the crossfader is assigned to your two CD channels, that the autostart terminals on the CD player are connected to the autostart terminals on the relevant channels of the mixer and that the crossfader is engaged. Next, use the crossfader to trigger the sample by bringing it into a central position, then re-cue the sample by bringing the crossfader back into its original position. This method is far less fiddly than the 'play/cue' technique, and you can move the crossfader much faster.

Alternatively, the relevant channel faders can be used for the same purpose by engaging the fader start switches under the CD channel faders and disengaging the crossfader.

By using the crossfader to trigger the selected sample or stab, you can make much quicker or more complicated patterns with them. With a bit of practice, a voice sample can even be made to sound transformed and is especially brilliant if a tone CD is used. (A tone CD is a CD that has been burned specifically for DJ tricks. It has long synth tones at various pitches ranging from low to high. By using the crossfader autostart feature, the tones can be triggered to play a rhythmic pattern over the other track in play.)

Final Scratch

How many times has a DJ looked out across the dance floor and wished that he or she had a particular tune? One that would put the crowd right where they wanted them and made the dance floor really jump?

Of course, the worst problem for the traditional vinyl-playing DJ is that carrying any more than 200 vinyl records requires staff. But this means your set suffers, because you can't always travel with the volume of material you would ideally wish for.

So, DJs began to gain interest in computers. But, as computer DJ software developed through the '90s, it tended to take on the look of a pair of CD players side by side on the screen, and everyone knew all along that, for DJs to take MP3 seriously, they would need to be able to drive the system with far more control than a mouse could offer.

So, with this in mind, manufacturers finally began to develop a range of outboard hardware accessories to add to the growing range of software. Rack-mount controllers that plug into the computer now offer everything you would get with dual CD players – the ability to cue a track at a press of a button, start a track playing, pause, scroll, search and add effects – but all via dedicated buttons.

As you know so well by now, serious DJs need the traditional tactile vinyl, but they also need a format that can be manipulated in real time to allow for latency issues in computer music production. Not to mention that most worthwhile DJ tricks require vinyl.

So, thank God a couple of Dutch guys hit on a genius idea. They thought to themselves, 'What if, instead of embedding music in the grooves of a vinyl 12-inch, we embedded a time code that could be read by a computer?'

Here, a time code is a constantly counting clock which we're all familiar with as the numbers running at the bottom of a music video on MTV. As the needle passes through the groove of the time-coded vinyl, it sends that clock information to your computer, which then maps that information to a tune you've selected from your database. In this way, the selected tune responds accordingly – as you move the vinyl on the deck, the computer plays the music. Spin it fast and the computer plays the music fast. Spin it slow and the computer plays the music slow. Stop = stop. Jiggle = jiggle. It actually is a vinyl controller.

Bpm-matching is done in the same way as traditional mixing – that is, by listening through the headphones and adjusting the pitch of the turntable. Tactile deck manipulation also remains the same. The performance of the DJ effectively remains the same, too, only the DJ is afforded the opportunity to select music from a massive digital database of music – by genre, bpm, artist, title, remixer, label, wa'eva. Free at last, free at last, free at last...

In early 2001, a group of technicians and DJs started to investigate the deeper aspects of digital-domain DJing. They simultaneously set off on a mission to establish which laptop computers would work best in very demanding touring situations and under heavy club use. They developed custom accessories to overcome many issues (especially in protecting computers from accidental drink spillages).

With the endorsement of Stanton Magnetics (the licence holders of the Final Scratch product), Switch52 was launched. Switch52 started out building custom systems for professional DJs. Seb Fontaine and Maxi Jazz of Faithless were among the first to begin using them live. These systems came road-ready and the DJ didn't have to configure any software.

Many pro and amateur DJs are now adopting this technology. The accelerated pace of development means that new developments are emerging all the time. For the latest information, visit www.stanton-magnetics.com or www.switch52.com. It's worth noting that Switch52 specialises in DJ software and that they have plenty of information about all the main players in this field.

 DJ Tips

Before buying a laptop for DJ use, check that the software is compatible.

MPEG

In 1987, a company called the Moving Picture Experts Group developed a very powerful algorithm that took advantage of the strange way human ears perceive sound. By removing the sounds or frequencies on an audio track that the human ear cannot normally hear (in most situations), the developers were able to reduce dramatically the storage space required. This meant that far more data could be stored in a smaller space or on a smaller disc, or could be streamed more easily over the Internet. The algorithm used was so efficient and useful that it was quickly adopted as the industry standard for digital music. Thus, MPEG was born.

When MP3 was being touted as the new industry standard, a company appeared called Nullsoft which created a clever piece of software that gave the user a way of playing back MP3 files in any chosen order – a kind of mini home jukebox. Nullsoft named this piece of software WinAmp (and the company ended up being sold a few years later for upwards of $80 million).

MP3 hit the headlines of the tabloid press a few years later when it was celebrated for superseding pornography in Internet downloads, or 'hits'. Hailed as a cheap and easy medium for distributing music over the Internet, MP3 was supposed to ignite the sales of 1,000 hopeful bands, all of whom could now retail their music to new and directly accessible armies of fans.

However, downloading music by bands you'd never heard of was quickly overtaken by downloading music by bands you *had* heard of and wanted to listen to, and the music moguls became very angry indeed. Everybody say 'Napster'.

Due to its small file size, its high-quality sound and the ease with which files could be shared via the Internet, computer owners all over the world were filling their machines with hundreds of their favourite music titles. Almost any track a surfer could desire was available for free and ready for immediate download and playback.

Marketing companies flaunted the music copyright laws in order to attract large amounts of consumer traffic to websites. Legal battles began and record labels recoiled at the thought of potential lost revenues. As soon as one MP3 music-sharing site was closed down, two more would pop up to replace them. Chatrooms became the new cafés where web-savvy music lovers swapped information about the latest places to obtain free music. Music moguls were helpless – they could do little to stem the flow of music swapping that took the Internet by storm. This music revolution was consumer-led, saw no boundaries or international borders and attracted people from all ages and countries.

The music industry is now quick to lay the blame for slumping record sales at the door of MP3. For the first time, the large companies were sidelined in the development and sales of a new music-storage format. At first, they devoted millions to legal challenges and little to embracing the new frontier that lay ahead. MP3 had gained a huge army of loyal followers, including the record company's greatest assets: recording artists. Of course, sooner or later they had to accept that MP3 music files were here to stay and develop new business models that could embrace the format.

Soon, DJ software developers in both Europe and the US unveiled custom programs that enabled computer users to play back two MP3 files simultaneously with clickable options to speed up or pitch-shift MP3 files, bpm match, add EQ and effects plus all the usual features you'd expect in a DJ-booth environment. The cat is now truly out of the bag and computer-based home DJs from all over the world can have a go at beat mixing.

The explosion, as you well know, is fast paced and ever-evolving. If you already own a computer and it is connected to the Internet, you can browse the free downloads for DJs that litter the Web. Log on to www.switch52.com and try out several different free-to-download music-mixing software programs.

The Science Behind MP3

The object of the MP3 format is to compress a song by a factor of ten or more without losing the apparent sound quality. With MP3, a 32MB (megabyte) song on a CD compresses down to about 3MB. Pointedly, this means that downloading music via the Internet takes minutes rather than hours.

The big question is, 'Is it really possible to compress a song by so much without seriously affecting the real sound quality?' Well, no, but by using a technique called *perceptual noise shaping*, the MP3 format uses the characteristics of the human ear to design the compression algorithm. It's complicated mathematics without a doubt, but, put simply, the algorithm is doing the following:

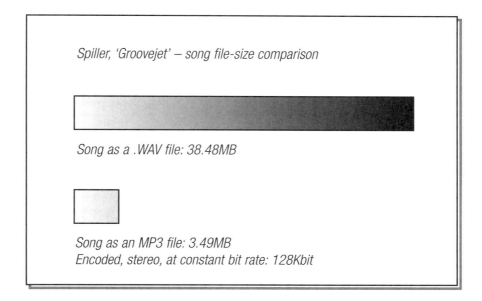

Spiller, 'Groovejet' – song file-size comparison

Song as a .WAV file: 38.48MB

Song as an MP3 file: 3.49MB
Encoded, stereo, at constant bit rate: 128Kbit

MP3 and .WAV comparison chart

- Firstly, it removes the extreme frequencies which the human ear doesn't normally hear.
- Next, it checks whether two sounds are playing at the same time, removing the quieter one, if so.
- Finally, it compresses the remaining data using standard computer compression methods (similar to Zip).

The PC: Mixer, Amp, Speakers

Most personal computers now come with a reasonable-quality soundcard ready installed. (Really, they all do, but some are more reasonable than others.) A soundcard translates the digital music file back into the audio that the human ear understands. It also acts as an amplifier so that you can plug speakers in and listen to the music, as you would a stereo.

The PC, of course, is capable of running many different applications, and many different DJ software products are available for home computers. The graphical user interface (what the user sees on the screen) tends to represent two identical record players side by side with a mixer desk underneath and a music list or record box under that. So the whole DJ package – the full monty – is usually on one screen. No separate

decks, mixer, records, CDs, amplifiers, needles or any other part of the normal DJ set-up are required.

If you already own a home computer, this is by far the cheapest way to start DJing. The software can be downloaded for free from the Internet and is even given away on the backs of some packets of cereal. Once loaded, you'll be able to play any of the music files stored on your computer or downloaded from the Internet. The software will offer a pitch shifter to enable the tunes to be bpm-matched and a mixer desk to fade tunes in and out. The player music information is usually displayed in a shaded or off-coloured box and includes track name and bpm, track running time and time remaining.

Some of the better software packages will also offer a BVPM engine that will calculate the exact bpm of your entire music collection and other features, such as cue-point editing, on-board effects and music looping.

To mix properly using a computer, however, you will need to be able to pre-fade listen to a track prior to playing it out of the speakers – just as is required on a full hardware set-up (so beware of cheap versions that don't provide this feature). Although it should be noted that each software manufacturer designs its products slightly differently (so experimentation and a thorough reading of the owner's manual is essential), there are three ways of doing this:

- For the first method, only a standard soundcard is required. Plug the headphone jack in the left-hand speaker output and the speakers in the right-hand speaker output. Now configure the software to send the cue audio to the left-hand channel and the main output to the right-hand channel. The true stereo signal will be lost, but that shouldn't stop you having fun.

- The second method requires a soundcard with front and rear outputs. Plug the headphones into the front speaker output of the soundcard and the speakers into the back output. Configure the software to send the cue audio to the front output of the soundcard and main audio to the rear outputs. This method retains the stereo signal.

- In the third method, two soundcards are required, and the software configuration will consist of sending the cue signal to one soundcard and the main output to the other.

With the first two options, you can configure the software to send two separate stereo signals to a separate external mixer. The benefit of having an external mixer is that the DJ has a more tactile surface to work with. Less time is spent pointing a mouse to bring up the volume in the headphones.

Cueing/Playing/Pitching

Some software manufacturers, such as PCDJ and VisualDisco Mix, have created external hardware components to avoid having to chase a mouse around the screen. They enable the user to select a tune, cue it up and start it using a separate hardware device.

When cueing using a computer, the first drum beat of the tune must be located as normal. Press Play until you hear the first beat and then press Cue. Now, using whatever method is afforded by the software manufacture, manipulate the track backwards and forwards in slow motion until the very first sound of the very first drum beat can be heard. Once you've

found the first drum beat, press Cue again. The tune is now cued and ready to play. Quite often in Cue or Edit modes, the software repeats the first fraction of the sound it's playing, which creates a 'da-da-da-da' effect. Get used to recognising the sound of a kick drum in Edit mode to identify it more quickly.

Now start the tune playing, load up another song and cue it up in the same way. If the software enables you to match the bpm with the track already playing, do it now. At the end of the phrase of the track that's playing out, press Play and use the pitch-up (+) and pitch-down (–) keys to bring the two tunes in to sync.

DJ Tips

Music can suffer latency issues; in other words, it will wander in and out of sync on its own. To be ready for this, the mouse pointer must be left hovering over the + and – keys so you can rectify any anomalies quickly.

With all these packages, however, it remains a reality that actually dragging a normal home computer into a club is usually a horrible nightmare. Some manufacturers, such as www.switch52.com, build toughened laptop computers that are designed for club use and can withstand a lot of punishment. They also have a range of software and accessories designed to be used in demanding environments.

Digital Beat Matching

Beat matching using a digital system is done in the same way as vinyl beat matching. The phrasing of the tune must be examined and remembered (ie are there four beats to the bar and eight bars to the phrase?). The song being introduced to the mix must follow the same set of rules and start at a point at which it is synchronised to the tune already playing.

One software manufacture, www.visualdiscomix.com, has built a unique beat-matching engine and includes it in its software. The software pre-examines the beats (before they play) and locks them together. As long as the DJ presses Play at something resembling the right time in the phrase, it will do the rest of the hard beat-matching work automatically. Listening is believing – they seem to have created a unique piece of DJ software

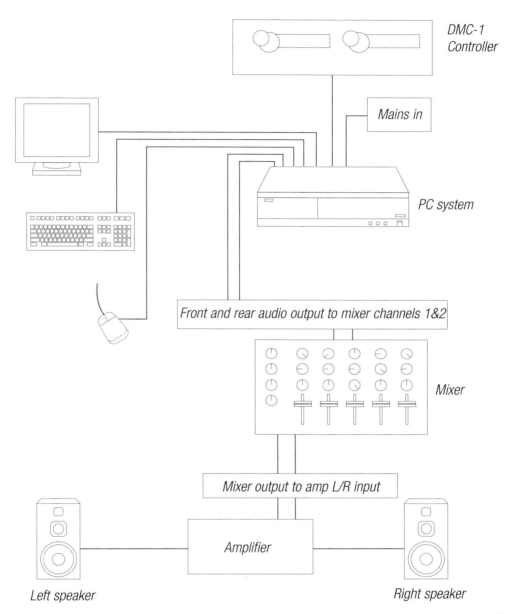

DMC-1
Controller

Mains in

PC system

Front and rear audio output to mixer channels 1&2

Mixer

Mixer output to amp L/R input

Left speaker

Amplifier

Right speaker

A typical PC set-up

that works brilliantly with both live mixing and remixing. Two selected tracks, once locked together, will stay that way for as long as you leave them playing. As an extra bonus, the software enables you to sample and loop individual parts of the track. A free download to try out the software is available at www.visualdiscomix.com or www.switch52.com

Ripping And Encoding

Ripping is the act of loading music from a source to storage medium (usually from the Web to your computer) and *encoding* refers to the level of quality at which the audio will be stored. Both are integral to the digital DJ set-up – if music software is set to store music at too low a quality or on an inappropriate

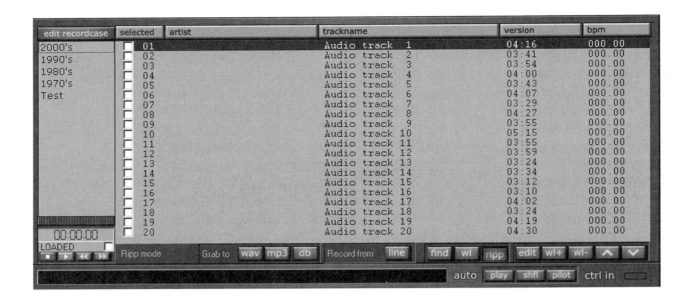

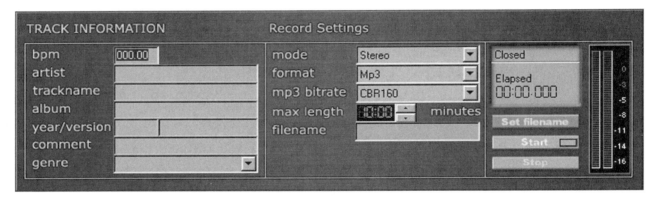

Top: PC DJ software shows a list of tracks from a CD that can be ripped and stored on a computer hard drive. Bottom: the software enables you to add track information

storage medium, it can be like listening to it through a Victorian telephone.

Start with a CD that you own and wish to load on to your computer for DJing. First, you'll require software that can rip – that is, glean the information from the CD, store it on your computer's hard drive and label it with an address so you can find it later. The software will offer you one or more format options in which to save the file. MP3, of course, is preferable because it compresses the size of the file so that many tracks can be stored without requiring a huge hard drive. The downside, as noted above, is that a slight loss of quality will be experienced, depending on the amount of compression applied. The minimum Kbps (kilobits per second) at which a DJ should consider encoding music for performance play is 192Kbps, while 256Kbps is strongly recommended. Saving at a higher ratio than that will only improve the sound quality.

The second method is called .WAV (referred to as 'dot wave'). This method transfers the music information without any compression, so if you want to save lots of tracks, you'll need lots of spare space on your computer's hard drive. On the plus side, mind you, .WAV files have next to no degradation in the quality stakes, but this will be of little consequence to all but the most ardent audiophiles.

Most software will walk the user through all the stages of ripping or loading a track from a CD to the computer. Follow the steps, ensuring that you've selected a reasonable bit rate for MP3 ripping.

Once loaded, the track will require labelling so it can be found again, this is usually called *IDV tagging*. Fill in as much detail as you can in the name, since all DJ software packages offer a search facility that enables you to find a track by any of the information you've attached to the IDV tag. Once saved, always play the tune back all the way through and listen carefully to make sure there are no glitches in the track. Now the track is ready for you to DJ with.

For safety reasons, it's always worth backing up your music onto a separate hard drive or data CD-ROM so that if, God forbid, something should go wrong, you'll still have the music tagged and ready to play.

If you own a collection of vinyl records, you may wish to add these to your computer music files. Obviously you can't jam a record into the tray of a computer like you can a CD, so a different method of loading the music is required. The first thing to note is that vinyl records use 'analogue' methods to store the music on the record: the music is cut into the groove as physical peaks and troughs. This will require translating into a binary code that the computer can understand. There are many devices that will do this and will go in-line between the turntable and the computer soundcard. One particularly good device is the Numark TTX turntable, which has a digital line output built in, thereby making the whole operation simple.

Once the turntable is connected to the computer, by whatever method you choose, follow the same steps as for ripping a CD to record your vinyl tracks. Once they're loaded, they may require you to edit any silence from the front of each recording. Any basic editing software product will be able to achieve this goal easily and quickly.

When resaving the newly edited track, be sure to check that the sample rate is high enough for your needs.

On-line Databases

The ability to bring all your music into one space for cataloguing offers a huge benefit for DJs. The DJ is now able to search at high speed through mountains of

The Play page for MP3 software, showing timings of the tune and the other necessary controls for mixing

Two DJ mixing stations and one recording station nestled together highlight the ever-increasing interplay between DJing and recording

music to locate a desired track by using a number of different search methods such as song title, duration of track, artist, remixer, and so on. However, as your library of music grows, so it will require maintenance and management. This section of the book is important to anyone planning on going mobile with file-based music, as failure to manage music content can be an expensive and time-consuming error.

As mentioned earlier, by far the most popular computer storage medium for music is MP3, which allows many thousands of tracks to be stored on a modern domestic computer. But for any of those tracks to be of use, the DJ will need to be able to locate them quickly, so it's crucial that you name your music files appropriately.

Most music software packages offer the function of naming a track, and it is likely to be called an IDV tag. The tag is a part of the MP3 file at the start that is able to store reference data. This data is then permanently attached to the music file and will remain attached even if you make a back-up copy on a separate hard drive. Fill in as many of the fields as you can, as each field can be searched to help you locate music, and then carry out a process that's as important as the original loading of the track: back up the music on a spare hard drive used only for your music. If you use an iPod (Apple's portable device that brilliantly stores thousands of tracks), back it up onto a hard drive that doesn't leave the house and doesn't get used for gaming or any other job. The music library must remain sacred and pure – it's not to be lent out to friends.

One day – and that day will come – the computer hard drive will develop a problem and the music you've spent hours recording, labelling and filing suddenly won't be available to you. Only at that point of no return will you realise that backing up the music in full was a must-do.

So, when you've recorded, named and stored your digital music files ready to play out, the last thing to do is organise them into 'virtual record bags'. With digitally stored music, it's easy to go a bit mad at first and find that you have every album you've ever bought on the hard drive – that's 3,500 tunes, of which 3,200 you'll never play.

Therefore, organising the music is important. Searching through every Fatboy Slim track to find the one you want to play is counter-productive. Exactly how the search operation takes place depends on which DJ software package you've opted for, so virtual record bags will help to keep things tidy. The obvious way – and the tried-and-tested way – is to group genres of music together. For example, all the chillout tunes can be arranged together so they can all be pulled from one box, and so on.

Most DJ software allows for tunes to be in more than one 'record box' at a time: a chillout tune with a slight funky beat can be put in the Funky record box as well as the Chillout box. With such a doubling up, the comment box could include the words 'crossover' so that you know it can be used to cross from Chillout to Funky Beats, and vice versa. The comment box will appear when you're naming the track in the IDV tag area.

Keep a system going of how your music is commented – for example, 'strings' would indicate that, whatever genre of music, it has a string section.

Using of these sorts of labels – such as 'piano' and 'guitar' – will make the job of choosing a suitable tune to mix that much easier. But keep it simple when it comes to the comment box; you don't need the British Library collection system on the road.

With all the music fully named and placed in suitable virtual record boxes, it just leaves you to check through them. Remove tunes from your 'working' record boxes – the record boxes that are used at gigs – and place the music in a separate box, perhaps marked 'Personal Music'. This sort of idea will give your eyes and mind less work on the night, as you won't be reading the names of classical pieces that you have no intention of playing.

Removing, or *culling*, tunes from the database is as important as adding them. The goal is to end up with different-genre record boxes that contain only the music you want to play and, ideally, no duff tunes. Of course, there are millions of places on the Internet to get music, for free or as a paying customer, but the biggest scare is in the quality of the audio. On-line file-sharing users tend to offer lower-bit-rate recordings than one would like to use as a pro DJ, and these tracks often have bizarre edits at the end – sometimes the track just stops because it has been lifted from a mix album.

The other main danger is the risk of downloading a bug along with a tune. The best option is to load your own music (which is legal) and not file-share it with anyone. That way you know that the music in your virtual record boxes is of good audio quality and contains no bugs, which tend to appear in the middle of a set.

More and more retailers have moved toward offering music files on-line, and the cost should be fairly modest (how else will they stop file sharing?). This will mean that the DJ will be able to buy music that is recorded well, fully labelled and free from bugs, all at a reasonable cost.

8 PLAYING OUT

'Being a good DJ doesn't make you a good promoter and being a good promoter doesn't make you a good DJ. Unless you're Dave Beer, of course.' Danny Whittle, director, Pacha, Ibiza

Once you've learned to mix and have put a steaming box of tunes together, it's time to start looking for work. With new bars and clubs opening all the time (and yes, they are), there's always a demand for DJs who can keep a venue full. Getting a foot in the door can seem impossible, but persistence pays off. Be ready for rejections, because it happens – that's life. (Remember to politely ask for a reason for the rejection, as it's always worth trying to find out where improvements can be made.) Clubs, weddings, birthdays and company functions are also 'gigs', though how much you charge for these events may vary quite widely; it depends on how many hours you're expected to play, what equipment you need to supply and how far you have to travel.

There's no easy way of getting a gig: a budding DJ must talk to everyone he meets. Leave no stone unturned but, at the same time, try not to be a pain in the arse going about it. Send your CD to every promoter and booking agency within a 20-mile radius and then, a week later, call the office and ask if they listened to the CD. Keep all the addresses and phone numbers in a database so you can send out a fresh mix every month. This will show them that you're serious, determined and able to keep it together. Also, try to enter every DJ competition available, whether it's a held in a magazine, on the radio or on-line.

Word Of Mouth

If a friend proclaims a new coffee shop on the high street as the best coffee shop he or she has ever visited, chances are you'll pay it a visit. However, if the coffee shop ran a full-page advert claiming to serve the best coffee in the coolest environment, the chances

are that you'll assume they're exaggerating. Likewise, the most effective way of securing DJ work is by word of mouth.

If a possible lead is passed on to you, contact the person quickly. Explain what you do and try to get a face-to-face meeting. (Make those calls now before someone else does and beats you to the job.) Ask friends – in fact, ask everyone you meet – if they know of any promoters. Always be ready to play a gig and make sure everyone knows what style you play. All too often people get let down by DJs, so if you're always ready and willing to play the gig, you'll be in the best position to get more bookings from the promoter.

Always carry plenty of business cards, demo tapes and personal biographies around with you at all times – one day you may be surprised by someone that you know that knows someone's brother that knows someone in the industry and may well be happy to help secure you a gig.

Making A Demo CD

It's now expected of a DJ that he should have a little bit of himself to give away to every potential customer in the form of a mix tape. People seem to think that a DJ without a demo must be an amateur, so you've got to have one. You've also got to be prepared to spend money creating it, and you'll have to give it away free. Often.

The easiest and cheapest way to make a demo is simply to record yourself in action. The goal is to record your best-ever set, but this is rarely achieved, so most will settle for a quite-good set. If you're able to record yourself playing out several times, you may be lucky enough to (accidentally) capture a particularly inspired performance, but more likely you'll have to record at home.

To record your set in a club, you need only to find yourself some kind of recording machine and connect its inputs to the master outputs on the venue's mixer (ask the club's engineer, if possible). It's acceptable to record yourself on tape – even a cassette machine, if no other options exist – because the loudness of most dance music tends to mean that any tape hiss can't be heard. A better option would be a recordable CD machine, but these are expensive and friends don't tend to let you take their dad's machine to a smoke-filled club with flying beer.

A more realistic option is to record yourself at home. In such a controlled environment, you're more likely to have a decent machine loaned to you, or, better still, you might get hold of a computer program for recording audio (or a music program like Cubase) which would enable you to record digitally.

But don't spend too much time worrying about the format: people don't tend to care about the quality of the sound if the choice of music is right and the mixing is good.

The ideal demo CD should be a one-hour continuous mix that shows off your best mixing, contains one or two tasteful tricks and is technically faultless. The tunes must build during the mix so as to create a one-hour set that makes musical sense, with a beginning, a middle and an end.

If you do record at home, it's crucial that you somehow catch enough of a vibe that the mix should sound inspired. Do whatever it takes to recreate the conditions necessary for this to occur. Keep trying as many times as necessary, even over several weeks, to get it absolutely right. Your finished product should be your favourite album.

Once you do manage to create a master tape or disc containing your demo, you'll need to copy it onto a few CDs. Until recently, this meant paying a studio or a copying company upwards of £10 ($16) per CD, but not any more; it's now virtually impossible that you can't think of a parent or a sibling or a friend or a mad auntie that doesn't have a computer with a CD writer. With these little babies, CDs should cost you no more than £1 ($1.60) a pop.

Remember to put your contact name and number on the CD itself and not just on the cover, as covers tend to get separated from discs. If you use a wild stage name, write your real name next to your phone number, as a promoter may feel a bit self-conscious about dialling a number and asking for DJ Eight-Legged Spider Man.

Print up the best possible graphics for the cover so as to separate you from all the other DJs who have only handwritten covers and discs. Keep the graphics simple and make sure they reflect your style of music. Make your CD serve as a business card, with words that are easy to read and understand. If you're feeling brave, use a photo of yourself for the front cover.

Marketing

Marketing yourself is essential if you want promoters and potential clients to know you exist. Some of the best DJs in the world forever remain mixing to the bedroom wall because they never make a noise about how great they are. Here are a few tips to help with marketing yourself.

Business Cards

Business cards are essential to give to friends and people who will want to be able to contact you for future bookings, and don't be tight when handing them out. Keep the design relatively simple so that it can easily be read, and be sure that it includes one line of text explaining what you do. Make sure that all of your contact details are on the front.

Local Newspapers

Let your local newspaper know what you're doing. Local papers need local news, and they'll write a story about you if you can find an interesting angle. (Think about what your unique selling point is – perhaps you're a 'future success story' after taking a small business loan to set up as a DJ? Maybe you're very young and will make a feelgood-factor story, or perhaps you have a massive record collection that would make a great photo – keep thinking.) If nothing else, you could even just cold-call a local journalist and offer your services for their next function. There are some basic rules for journalism and potential stories are judged by some pretty ridiculous criteria:

- **Celebrities** – If you're DJing at a party attended by an even vaguely well-known guest, then you may be news;
- **Money** – the bigger the number, the bigger the story;
- **Places** – a party in a slightly unusual location might be news.

For better or for worse, that's how the local press works – for print, the Internet, television and radio. Always carry a loaded camera in case a gig provides a photo opportunity that could turn into free publicity for you as a DJ. (Should Kate Moss show up at a party with you as DJ, politely ask if you could stand next to her for a photo, and try to get one with your DJ equipment in the background.)

The Web

A web page is a living business card. If the cost of setting up your own site is prohibitive, try teaming up with a few others. Keep the site simple and put the contact details up front with a photo of you in DJ guise. A testimonial from a past client or two and a sample set list also helps. And be prepared to travel, because the World Wide Web is just that – worldwide. If you're interested only in customers within a 20-mile radius, don't spend weeks planning an award-winning site. Potential customers want to know that you're reliable, have the right music and can mix. Keep it in mind that you're being paid to play music for others' entertainment, so add less about what you like and a lot more about what you can do for clients.

Free Listings

This includes local telephone directories, local press, boards and sites in record shops, Internet lists, library and church bulletins, and so on. Get your name and a brief description of what you do in as many as possible – and take note of the date you'll need to renew.

Networking

Organisations are everywhere and every organisation is a potential agent (or even a potential customer) for you. As part of your planning, you should draw up a list of local club promoters and organisations to which you can offer your services. The more people are aware of your service and know how to get in contact with you, the more work you'll get. Make friends with the club managers of all the local venues. They constantly receive phone calls from people wanting to book their venues for parties or club nights, and if the manager of another venue can recommend you, the chances are they will take his or her advice.

Radio

People do listen to the radio, and even the smallest station has listeners who are already fans of the music. There will always be a local or pirate radio station near you, and it's always worth trying to call up to find out who runs it. If you get lucky, try to arrange a meeting. If they agree to a meeting, listen carefully to the station beforehand and work out what they do well and what they do poorly.

Think of some simple ideas you could bring to the station, but keep it simple – it's no good offering a live broadcast from your next gig if you don't own an outside broadcast truck and a team of producers and engineers to make it happen. Maybe offer a specialist chart compiled by yourself, as a regional DJ, or by the local record shop, or by people emailing or texting you. If you know any local bands or musicians, you might offer to try to get interviews.

Personal Biography

When marketing yourself by post, it always helps to present a biography or a press release containing your own personal details and some interesting aspects of yourself that others might find interesting. Every CD or card you give out should also have a one-page, one-sided A4 information sheet to assist people who know little or nothing about you or your music. It should be easy to read and contain only information that is relevant to your life as a DJ and your music. Here's a helpful example:

Drum 'n' Bass DJ JOHN DOE

South London drum 'n' bass DJ John Doe has been spinning tunes for more than seven years. He has played his own sexy style of d'n'b all over the UK, including Leeds, Scotland and his hometown, London.

The crowd love him and the dance floor jumps to his unique sexy style.

DJ John Doe has now found time in his busy DJ schedule to get his hands dirty in the studio, where he is working on his next track. Described as 'cute' by the ladies, his appeal is never-ending. John has already been tipped by music writers as the next big thing to come to the scene and is looking forward to rocking even more dance floors in 2004.

To book DJ John Doe, call ACME Management on...

This example is something a promoter or magazine can work with to understand John and what he does. Notice how it's not like a CV; don't include hobbies or unrelated jobs or pastimes, and make sure it makes you sound good and, at the same time, professional.

Managers

A manager can be a handy person to have around, someone to do the footwork in finding gigs, handle the unpleasant paperwork, collect the dirty money and chase the villains. The trouble is, of course, a good manager is hard to find.

Typically, a manager takes 20 per cent of whatever you earn. If they're actually finding you the gigs, then it's a good deal. There is a school of thought, however, that says no manager of a DJ could ever get a gig that the DJ himself could not get – that is, you get the gigs because you're good and well known, not because someone else knows how to talk. The real answer is somewhere between the two; you need to be a good DJ already with at least some experience before you can ever get any gig, but you also need a bit of luck in timing the offers and marketing yourself, so a good manager needs both good luck and a good client.

The most important factor in any DJ/manager relationship is the relationship itself. If you don't trust him, don't respect him and, most importantly, don't have any confidence in him, don't make the mistake of letting him manage you.

Agencies

There are many kinds of agency that could potentially find you gigs. National agencies tend to be very hard to join and may be impossible without a personal connection. If you decide to sign up with a local one, request testimonials from other DJ clients to be sure that the company is what it seems. Being on the books of a busy agency could be a dream if they actually do keep you working and take care of the client bookings and collect the money for you.

The reality of many agencies, however, is that they do 90 per cent of their work for three core DJs and the other ten DJs have to share out a few low-paying, distant gigs. This arrangement is perfect if you manage to become one the core DJs, but this is difficult and usually takes some time. Be wary of any offer of an 'exclusive' agency, as this might mean that you're obliged to give up 20 per cent of money earned from all gigs, even when the agency has no involvement.

Agents often make a charge to add you to their books. First, ask about exactly what publicity they can get you, how many local DJs they have on their books and how many bookings they expect to find you.

As with managers, if you don't like the people running the agency and you don't trust and respect them, the chances are they're not worth your time.

Doing Your Own Night

One sure-fire way of getting a gig is to run your own night, but there are loads of issues to think about and questions to be answered before jumping in headfirst.

Before you pick up the phone, think about why you want to put on a night – and think long and hard on this one. In an ideal world, you would have to put on your own night because so many people want to dance to your style of music and are begging you to do it, but in the real world it's a lot of work and you'll need enormous determination to succeed.

Making a night a success will take careful planning and execution. Aside from those on the inevitable guest list, you must have confidence that enough people can be found to fill the venue.

You'll need to invite personally three times more people than the venue can hold in order to have even a hope of filling it. If the venue sells out, that's fantastic – you can't beat a queue of people trying to get into your night because it's so popular. A good promoter needs to socialise, so on the night, as well as DJing, you'll need to find time to meet and greet

Pro DJs keep the dance floor moving

all the guests. Make them feel special and thank them personally for turning up.

Publicity

Without adequate publicity, the night will fail, so every possible stop must be pulled out to get the word around. Fliers need to be printed to advertise the night, and they should reflect, in some way, the style of music and vibe you're trying to create. Cosy up to anyone you might know in the local press for all the free or discounted press you can get. Hand out fliers to everyone you meet and get friends to hand them out for you. And after your first night, try to build a database of people that came so it's easy to invite them to the next one.

Employees

You can't do a night alone. The minimum staff would probably be bar staff, a few hosts and, of course, other DJs will need to be hired in to cover – and they will

have to know exactly what style of music to play and, along with the others, must be paid.

Security

Security is normally organised by the venue, but be sure to ask a few questions before accepting that everything will be all right on the night: how aggressive are the door staff? Has there been much trouble in the past at the venue? Will your night be exclusive for your guests or will they be letting in other people that may conflict with the theme of the night?

Most security staff nowadays understand that working on the door of a venue is not an excuse to beat people up, but some still revel in the spoils of war and are looking for any excuse to break a nose or two. Meet the head of security and talk about what might be considered 'intolerable'. Ask if guests get searched on the way in and, if so, what they can expect and how far they'll go. Security is a crucial issue that has far-reaching effects. You can't be too careful.

Venue

A good venue needs to be the right size. It needs a good location, tight security, decent rental prices and to carry all the necessary licences.

Choose a venue that's just big enough for the event so that it looks full. Nothing is more off-putting than an empty event – you can always move on to a larger venue if the night sells out every time while the queue is still long. The location is important, as no one wants to travel all day to get to a gig. Ideally, the venue should have public transport access and parking.

Money

The cost of a venue can be calculated in several different ways. Some let you keep the takings on the door while the venue keeps the takings at the bar. Some venues set a lower limit so that, if not enough people show up on the night, you're expected to make up the shortfall. Other venues might require a flat fee. Whatever the proposed arrangement, try to think it through as far as possible so as not to miss the hidden catch – and inevitably, there's a hidden catch.

Sound Systems

If the venue has a sound system already installed, be sure to test it fully before you book. Listen carefully for distortion in the sound and check that the equipment isn't too worn out or in desperate need of replacing. Ask the manager how often the sound system is overhauled, if it has failed before on a night, and what happens financially if it should fail, causing the party to end early. A club might have a room full of spares and back-up equipment that can be thrown together to get things going again, but remember that you must also have someone on hand who knows how to do it, and it's most likely to happen at 2am.

Buying and owning a sound system is expensive and cumbersome. Storage is required when the system isn't in use and suitable transport is needed to get it to the venue. Once at the venue, it needs setting up and EQing (and then de-rigging at 4am).

If a venue doesn't have the sound system you require, renting is by far the easiest way to go, as often the rental company will set up, test and de-rig the equipment for you. Most will service the system on a regular basis and can adjust a set-up to suit the particular venue. And, if you hire from one company regularly, you should be able to negotiate a discount.

Still enthusiastic? Not put off quite yet? Well, if you have the necessary commitment to deal with all these issues, and still have enough energy left to do a good set, running a night can be a hugely rewardingly experience. On the other hand, when everything goes wrong – at once – it can also be the worst nightmare from hell. You pays your money and you takes your choice...

9 MAKING YOUR OWN TUNES

'When you're really starting out, it's better to get a mate to big you up in the clubs and present your mix tapes rather than try to do it yourself.' Dave Pearce, DJ and Radio 1 presenter

Nobody knows more about records than DJs. So, it's only natural that DJs should make records themselves. Even if you've only just started DJing, it won't be long before you too decide to DIY.

DJs generally make excellent record producers because they have so much practice in listening and judging records. A producer's job is basically just quality control: he decides if each and every idea and addition to the record actually makes it better or not. The producer, like the DJ, ensures that the listener gets the most bang for his buck.

The DJ business is the music business is the DJ business. We're all in the same game and it's called 'selling your music to scrape a living' – only, if anything, DJs have wider scope and more options and potential for making money out of music than the old music-business cronies themselves. Dance-music fans are not fussy about how they get their music: it could be the traditional ten-track CD of original songs, or one track mixed ten times, or one track mixed once lasting one hour, or old tunes mixed over each other, or new tunes mixed over old and new. If it feels good, do it – the masses might just buy it.

Recording And Producing Music

The world of recording is usually unknown to new DJs, but that never stops them. In fact, it's a serious advantage in that taking it on as a 'blind adventure' can make it far more exciting and inspirational, not to mention the benefit of not being constrained by all the traditional (tired) rules.

The first and most daring decision for a DJ wanting to make his own tunes is whether to stick to computers and decks or to strike out into the world of actual live

recording. Live recording means microphones and, more scarily, live performances with real instruments or voices. Obviously, working with live performers is a bit trickier than computer programming, but it's a lot more exciting and a more distinctive sound is likely to result – which is, after all, probably the most important factor in gaining a record-buying fan base.

The Studio In Your Computer

No matter what you choose as a basis for your tunes, these days the starting point (and the finishing point) is your PC. (Macs are, in fact, better tools for recording than PCs, but due to the wild popularity of PCs, we will stick to PCs in this chapter. For both kinds of computers, the process is almost entirely identical.)

By far the most popular music-production software program is Steinberg's Cubase, and this package forms the basis for this chapter. (There are countless other programs which are shockingly similar.) Cubase loads directly onto your PC, after you've installed the special music card inside. No further connections are necessary, unless you choose to use a piano keyboard as an interface (to perform on) or a mic with which to record.

MIDI

Cubase is a MIDI-based program. MIDI (Musical Instrument Digital Interface) is the language that computers use to 'speak' music. Each note on the piano keyboard is given a number, starting with the bottom key (C1), which gets the number '1', and the computer refers to each note by its number. The various other factors that comprise a performance on the keyboard are also given coded numbers for the computer to recognise and record – for example, how loudly or softly you hit the keys (velocity), how fast or slow you play the song (tempo) and how long you hold down each note (duration). In this way, the computer can 'listen' to you play the keyboard (against a drumbeat or a click) and record the performance. Afterwards, the computer can play back exactly what you played or, more conveniently, it can automatically correct your mistakes in timing and play back a perfect (and often far more funky) performance. Thus, through the magic of computers, we can all be top-quality musicians.

The main page of Cubase is called the Arrange page, because it shows the full arrangement of one song horizontally, with each instrument set out in a vertical list. Within a few minutes of first tinkering with Cubase, most people will quickly and instinctively understand how the page is set out and easily locate the various parts (the drum part or the bass part) to edit. The Arrange page is so well set out that many successful Cubase programmers never actually bother to go beyond it, though there are many very useful pages underneath, such as the Key Edit page and the Note Edit page.

It must be understood, however, that MIDI is a system for recording performances only, not sounds. This means that, while you might choose to use a piano sound (from a separately bought and plugged-in free-standing synthesiser, for instance) to play your MIDI-recorded performance, you could always change your mind at a later point and decide to make the performance that you recorded as a piano be played on an organ or a clavinet instead. The upshot of this concept is that the process of MIDI recording and computer production is literally limitless. Your options never dwindle. Of course, this can be a nightmare just as easily, so a good producer needs to know when to quit.

'Nobody ever finishes a record. They just abandon it.' *David A Stewart, The Eurythmics*

So, the MIDI-based program Cubase is your tool for recording performances, but you'll also need some kind of sound source (musical instrument sounds) as well, and this means using synthesisers – either self-contained keyboard synths, such as the popular Yamaha M1, or computer-based synths, which are often

just software versions of the most popular keyboard synths. Whatever you choose, remember that you'll need a decent range of options for sounds, as too limited a range will quickly cause boredom and make all your tunes sound the same. An easy option would be simply to purchase a single rack-mounted box that has a wide range of sounds inside it – such as a Roland JV-80 – and plug the audio outputs into your sound system to hear all the weird and wonderful sounds that you can access inside it via the Cubase program and your keyboard as a controller.

Live Recording

After you've toyed around with Cubase and MIDI instruments for long enough, the time will inevitably come when you're ready for microphones. To record real instruments or voices, the first thing you need is something to record them onto, as MIDI sequencing packages record only MIDI performances – they physically cannot record the sound picked up by a microphone.

In the old days, the solution would have been a tape recorder – probably a four-track, cassette Portastudio. On those lovely old machines, you would use track 1 to record your drum track from a drum machine (by plugging the output of the drum machine to the input of the Portastudio and pressing Play/Record); next you would record your bass line on track 2 by connecting your bass synthesiser to the Portastudio, pressing Play/Record and manually playing the bass line in time to the already recorded drums, which you would be listening to from track 1. You would then record a piano bit onto track 3 in the same manner and, finally, record yourself singing into a microphone on track 4. This process of building up a tune track by track, always listening to what you've already recorded so far each time in order to hear how the next part works with the rest, is called *overdubbing* and is the basis for all traditional recording.

Computer music production is no different and never will be. Everyone starts by recording the basic rhythm track – sometimes just a 1-2-3-4 bass drum for six minutes or so – and then overdubbing the next part over the top (commonly the bass line). The only difference today is that you have so many choices of sounds to use. If you've done recording in the past

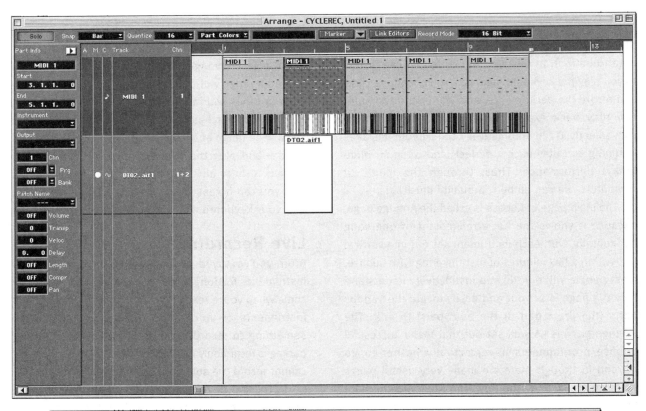

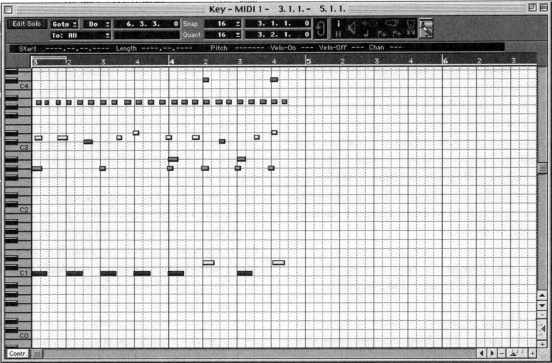

**The Arrange page (top) and Key Edit window
showing MIDI information in Cubase VST**

and you own an electronic keyboard of some kind, you might as well incorporate that into your Cubase set-up on your PC, as it's already there, and it'll give you another avenue for sounds straight away. If you own nothing yet, you're more likely to buy only one or two software sound modules and keep the whole operation inside your PC.

As Portastudios no longer exist, however, recording a performance on a microphone requires you to go the extra step beyond just the Cubase MIDI program and install a digital soundcard that enables you to record sound digitally simply by plugging the microphone into the computer, hitting Play/Record on your Arrange page and jamming.

Of course, whatever instrument you play or sing into the microphone will be recorded exactly as it is, and you could leave it that way for the natural vibe. But you won't. You'll decide to edit it. And you'll spend many, many hours editing it, because you want to make your own guitar performance sound like you hired Jimi Hendrix to come over to your front room for a session. And, in time, you will make it sound like that. Even if it kills you.

Editing digital recordings is pure magic. Using the cut-and-paste system you can correct any or all mistakes, or perhaps repeat that fabulous riff you did by accident in the last verse throughout the song. By using Antares' AutoTune program, you can correct any notes that were sung out of tune; by using the quantise function and a fair amount of digital chopping, you can make the entire performance fall perfectly into flawless – and seriously funky – timing. The possibilities are, again, literally endless.

The Bedroom Producer

For most DJ producers, Heaven is a personal combination of the above choices. Certainly it is best to have both the MIDI and the live recording kit installed, as well as a few old-school, free-standing synths lying around to offer a wide range of choices with which to indulge your creative urges. Some people, however, have produced the most fantastic records of the last few years using only a crude version of Cubase called Reason, which offers a very limited choice of sounds and editing possibilities. Since your budget is likely to be the controlling factor, the most important ingredients will therefore be time, determination and imagination.

Selling Records

Once you've made a record that you're happy with and the time comes for you to start trying to sell it, a good overall understanding of the business is an invaluable asset which can save you endless headaches and much wasted time.

The music business is fundamentally different from most businesses. Unlike everything else in the world (which is getting bigger every day), the music business is shrinking. But don't misunderstand: more and more records are sold every year. The 'business', however – the number of existing record companies – gets smaller. This explains why the charts have changed so much from their heyday and why they seem to matter far less.

To illustrate: when The Beatles had a Number One single in any given week in the '60s they would have sold something like 250,000 records in that seven-day period to gain the distinction of having the week's best-selling record in the UK. Contrast that with a typical Number One from 2003: in a low week (say, in August), the UK Number One might sell as few as 50,000 records. The main reason for this is that The Beatles were competing with only two or three dozen releases per week, whereas some weeks in 2003 saw nearly 1,000 records go on sale. So, as the choice increases and the sales spread around, the overall number of records shifted goes up while the sales for any one particular record drop.

The smaller numbers for chart sales means that the only way to earn huge money is to own a huge chunk of the chart on a regular basis – and this is why record companies have been so busy buying each other. There are now effectively only five record companies left controlling over 80 per cent of the music business, while the remaining 20 per cent is shared out by all the rest – the 'indie' labels of the world, each one of which is so tiny it couldn't even think about competing with the Big Boys. The five are: Sony, Warner (AOL Time Warner), BMG (the German Bertelsmann group), Universal (owned by the drinks company Seagrams) and EMI (the sole UK player, which is itself in constant danger of takeover by one of the others).

But all is not lost. In fact, this is good news for up-and-coming DJs producing records themselves – so long as they are aware of what the business now looks like and what the Big Five now want. What they want is low-cost product that has a ready-made market. Translation: you and yours. Dance music is easily made for a fraction of the budget of any other kind of music and comes complete with an audience because you, the DJ/producer, have been focusing on your audience since as far back as the first chapter of this book.

Record Labels And Record Deals

While the world has only five main record companies, each of those companies has many, many labels. A label is just a sub-division of a record company which tries to release only a certain kind of music and has a unique identity; nobody knows what an EMI record will sound like, but we all know what to expect from a Positiva record. So, the first step to getting a deal with one of the Big Five is to decide which of the hundreds of labels to target. This is usually an easy decision, since most DJs tend to target the labels that they are currently buying.

A record deal no longer means that the company gives you a small fortune to go away and make hits (and buy clothes and go on tour); the modern record deal means only that the company buys from the artist his master tape (or disc) and agrees to release it in some fashion. This means that all the development work, pre-production work, recording and mixing must be done by you – off your own back – before you ever face a label executive (still often referred to as an 'A&R man'). Furthermore, the size of the deal is unlikely to be more than a few thousand pounds or dollars, even if the cost of the studio – the computer, synths, mics, and so on – was twice that much.

The most important thing for you is getting the promise of a release. The most valuable thing a major label deal will provide is a 'major-label release', as this will almost certainly be an international one and will help to create a foothold for you in the business, whatever happens.

Publishers

It is important to distinguish between producing records and writing songs. 'Producing' a record refers only to the actual process of recording the performances (or the computer-generated sequences, as the case may be) and mixing them into an end product, while 'songwriting' refers only to the conceptual act of thinking up the notes (and the words, if there are any).

Record companies do not deal directly with songwriting, except insofar as they need to pay some songwriter to buy the rights for their own (signed) recording artists to record, copy and sell the songwriter's song. The songwriter will not be signed to a record company (unless he's a recording artist as well), but rather to a 'publisher' or 'publishing company'. Publishing companies are easily distinguished from record companies by the word *music* in their names: EMI Records would the company that signed The Beatles, while EMI Music would be the company that signed Lennon and McCartney as composers.

Just as a record deal gives an artist a cash advance to be getting on with while he records his music, and then pays him royalties on sales afterwards, a publishing deal gives a composer a cash advance to motivate him to write songs and then pays him royalties on whatever money the company generates from placing his songs in the market – usually by getting some band to record them and taking the publishing or 'writer's cut' from the band's record sales. In the old days, artists such as Elvis always recorded someone else's songs, and record companies and publishers needed to co-operate closely to keep Elvis' career fuelled. Since the '60s, however, many artists are whole packages, in that they write their own material, and the business has been made accordingly simpler. Of course, there are still many artists who enjoy success from recording other people's songs, producing what we know as *cover versions*.

If you should decide to record a version of an old song (or a new song, written by someone else), remember that you will need the permission of the writer in order to release it commercially. In practice, of course, no writer ever refuses such permission because, after all, that's their job and they need the work, so rest easy knowing that you can record

A typical small recording studio set-up featuring samplers, synths, a small mixer and various effect boxes

anything you want and, when the time comes, any record company that signs you or the record will take care of securing permission and paying the writer.

If, on the other hand, you can write your own songs, then a whole second front is open to you for financing your career. Publishing companies are always on the hunt for good writers and you must apply to them for a deal separately – with tapes, CDs, and so on – just as you would to a record company.

Publishing deals tend to be somewhat more difficult to get than record deals, as the risk to the publisher is greater, since the process of getting a record deal or of getting a different artist to record your songs must still be done and be ultimately successful. Nevertheless, there are plenty of publishers out there who are ready and willing to dole out wads of cash to budding songwriters early in their careers, and this can a very convenient way of staying financially afloat during the first (skint) part of your recording career.

If you have a reasonably successful DJing job, however, and you're able to get by on that alone, then you would be better off in the long run not signing a publishing deal since, even though they give you money up front, the publisher would, of course, take some percentage of your publishing royalties after any success. The later in your career that you sign a publishing deal, the more bargaining power you'll have and the higher the percentage of your own money you'll keep. If you're lucky enough to have success with your own recorded songs without having ever signed any sort of publishing deal whatsoever, then you'll keep 100 per cent of your publishing money – that is, your songwriting royalties.

Managers

Despite the crystal-clear picture of the music business that you gained from reading this book, you might still feel a desire to hire someone else to do your business for you. This would be understandable – not to mention that it would free you up to get on with the music. Furthermore, record companies and publishers can sometimes feel more comfortable and be impressed by dealing with a middle-man rather than with the artist himself.

Unfortunately, though, a good manager is as hard to find as a good record deal. All too often, managers will seem enthusiastic, excited and confident, only to become virtually invisible just a few months later. So it's important to choose a manager carefully and to be cautious about signing anything until you know who you're dealing with and what, exactly, the plan is.

Managers should always speak to people on both sides of the equation with record deals and publishing deals. There should always be a clear and reasonable timetable setting out times by which certain goals are to be achieved, and what happens if the goals are not achieved by certain times. Ideally, there should be some funding; when a manager puts his own money behind an act, he's far more likely to stick around longer and work harder to get it back. Remember that no money that any manager (or anyone in the business, for that matter) ever gives you should ever be refundable in any way, shape or form – except to be paid back out of royalties from records sold. The cash you get now is yours, now and forever.

It is important that a manager has a good understanding of your music (so that he knows how to sell it appropriately) and a good understanding of the existing record and publishing companies (so that he knows which ones are likely to interested in you

and your music). That way, no time is wasted on companies which would never sign you anyway. It's also important that a manager has a few contacts in the business, either to grease the wheels or for valuable advice on how to avoid pitfalls.

Most importantly, it is vital that your manager respects you and that a good level of trust exists. A manager would likely be your closest day-to-day co-worker and would have enormous power to act on your behalf. Rather like a marriage, if trust and respect aren't strong, the relationship could easily become harmful. Tread carefully.

Setting Up Your Own Label

DIY comes in two sizes: big and small. If your preferred size is big, then the process of running your own label is a lot of work. If your sights are small, it's hardly any bother at all. Running a record label means taking a finished master recording, mastering it (getting a professional mastering engineer to listen carefully and do a bit of finishing and polishing to make it sound like a record), pressing it up into masses of copies, distributing the copies (getting them physically into the shops) and promoting the product (getting people to buy copies).

In the small version, each of these tasks is really quite simple.

- **Mastering** – Mastering studios exist in every major city and are in the phone book. A typical mastering session for a single lasts about two hours and costs less than £500 ($800), including the cost of the 'master lacquer' (which you walk away with and from which the vinyl copies are pressed) and the digital master (from which the CDs are made). Whole albums tend to be about five times as much. You don't need to know anything about the process; just show up – and don't forget your cheque book.

- **Pressing** – Pressing plants are the factories that actually manufacture vinyl records and CDs stuffed into jewel cases. Any mastering studio could recommend a few for you to research and compare. The plant just receives your master lacquer or digital master (by post – no one ever actually goes there) and starts pressing copies. Prices follow the volume: if you press ten records, the price may be as much as £50 ($80) per copy, but if you press 10,000 records, the price may be as little as 50 pence (80 cents) per copy. Think about what you could realistically sell and then shop around.

- **Distributing** – Getting the records into the shops can be as easy as an overnight road trip. Many record shop owners are willing to carry a few copies of your record in their shops after just meeting you for five minutes at the shop's counter. Some shop owners will even pay you a bit on the spot and take the risk of selling your product, but

Lucy Ambache, DJ

more often they'll expect you to leave without paying and collect the money by post from any records that are sold. Don't be afraid to walk in and ask; it might help to bring some pamphlets, press releases, a biography or other publicity about the artist or the record or about yourself as a DJ. The hardest part is physically getting to all the different shops, which requires a car, a map and some petrol.

- **Promotion** – This is the trickiest bit, and even huge multinational record companies often get it wrong. There's an old saying: 'You know what happens if you don't advertise? Nothing.' And that just about sums it up. Of course, we all know the standard methods of promotion because we're all the target of the posters, fliers, handouts, freebies, newspaper, radio and TV adverts and radio and TV airplay. It's all part of promoting the record, 'selling the product' or 'moving units'.

  Maybe everything you do helps a little a bit and the combination makes success. Maybe just one method works and all the others are a waste of money. Maybe none of them works and success is just a fluke or good timing or dumb luck (or a good tune? Nah...). The only certainty is that, if no one knows it out there, no one can buy it.

  Of course, radio airplay does no harm, and has the added benefit of earning money for the artist and the songwriter every time the record is played. A radio station's Head of Music chooses the playlist on a weekly basis and their decision will be affected by people known as *pluggers*. Record companies regularly employ pluggers to secure airplay on radio (and MTV), so some sort of contact with a company would help you in finding a suitable one. Pluggers range in price from expensive (for effective ones) to cheap (for useless ones).

If you fancy having a go at selling fewer than 5,000 copies of your record in a single year then, as shown above, its not difficult, and you stand as good a chance of success as the next guy. If, however, you harbour higher hopes, then it's a full-time job – and a difficult one at that.

Running your own label on a bigger scale involves all the same fundamentals but requires a far higher success rate because the necessary investment is much higher in time and money. It is always tempting to order 50,000 copies of a record from the pressing plant instead of 5,000 because the price per record drops so dramatically (sometimes by more than a factor of ten), but the reality is that most record labels end up spending the money they initially saved by having to store the extra 40,000 records they ordered and paid for but now cannot sell. It's a dangerous trap which can become a short-term addiction (until the business finally goes bust), but it is easy to see why people fall into it (glamour, wine, sex, drugs, excitement, vanity, fun, boredom, unexpected windfalls, desperation and so on).

The lesson here should be clear: keep it functional. Don't press or invest any more than is strictly necessary or justifiable and, if at all possible, get someone else to pay for the lot.

Exploiting The Internet

So, the Web ain't what it was cracked up to be. There's now little chance of attaining dot.com millionaire status. Precious little music is being sold legitimately through websites, so no one's getting rich that way. Still, mustn't grumble...

Whether you intend to sell your records through your own label, sign a major deal or just sell mix CDs from the back of your white van, it's still a good idea to get webbed-up as soon as possible. Try to register as many variations of your intended name as possible and go for the highest level (ie '.com', '.co.uk' and even '.net'). Even if you can't afford to create a decent website or have no resources with which to sell on-line, you can always leave a phone number or postal address that may attract some custom. Furthermore, it's always an added benefit to a label or record deal to offer up your ownership of the domain name, and it could add a zero or two to the deal.

Sampling Or Stealing?

It is very likely that you, as a DJ, would make a record of your own using a sample from a different record. It's in our blood. It's what we do. We're DJs.

So, is it a crime? Well, no, it's not a crime, so don't worry about doing time, but there is a chance that it could cost you money. But don't just worry about it; rather, take a commercial view.

There was a joke a few years ago about an American DJ/producer who made a record which 'used and re-worked' the famous Michael Jackson classic 'Billie Jean' and he decided, in his DJ mixing brilliance that it didn't need anything else, and so released the record under his own name, which was simply the untouched 'Billie Jean'. It's a joke, but it cuts a bit close to the bone. Of course, if this had actually been the case, the record would have been nothing more than a cover version, or a remix at most, as it was mostly (or completely) someone else's record.

If you make a record that uses a sample (and adds some ideas of your own as well), then you may be infringing someone else's copyright and running the risk of being sued. If the other party should sue and win, you would stand to lose some or most of any profit that you made on your record using that sample.

So, to sample or no to sample? That is the question. There are four possible answers:

- Very small samples will cause no problems if they are virtually unrecognisable. The best example is the drum loop from a James Brown record affectionately known as the 'funky drummer'. A drum sound, a guitar twang or a piano chord is very unlikely to make your listeners think of the original record and cannot therefore be said to be a 'substantial copying' of the original and will not cause any legal problems. Remember that the decision is not based on the length of the sample but on the sample's importance, so while a long drum loop probably wouldn't be problem, a short vocal sample (like, say, from Black Box's 'Ride On Time') could very well be. It's all about the recognisability factor.

Assuming you've used a recognisable sample, there are now three possibilities open to you.

- If you intend your record to be only a white label, with only a few copies for playing out in your set and giving to friends, then it is incredibly unlikely – impossible – that the original composer will ever even know that you have done the naughty deed.

- If you intend to have a go selling your record on your own label, this answer lies in the numbers. If you press 20,000 copies of the single at a total cost of £20,000 ($32,500) and sell them all for £3 ($4.80) each and managed to spend as little as £10,000 ($16,250) on distribution and promotion, your net profit would be £30,000 ($48,800), a sweet addition to your annual DJing income. Then, if the original artist or composer should find out that your record exists, he would still be very unlikely to act. Copyright suits are difficult, uncertain and expensive and people do not spend so much money and time to gain so little. So don't worry about it. (Besides, even if you were sued, your settlement offer of £20,000 would be snapped up and you'd still have £10,000 and a great story to dine out on.)

- But, what happens if the unthinkable occurs – the record goes into orbit by selling bucketloads? If the initial run of 20,000 sells out and you decide to press another 80,000 and they all sell out, and then major offers come in for worldwide release and marketing, what now? In this case it seems likely that the original composer or artist (or his publisher) will find out and come knocking on your proverbial door, asking for non-proverbial money and threatening to file scary lawsuits in multiple countries. So, in this scenario, would you be screwed? Well, you'd clearly have to make huge settlement offers which might not be accepted and you'd be likely to have to part with hefty portions of whatever profits you might have made. But, is this really such a nightmare? You'd still be a top-selling artist/composer/label and you'd still have a tidy sum that you wouldn't have otherwise had and you'd still be in a position to make a follow-up single (without a sample this time) and you'd still have all the world's record companies desperate to sign you. So, don't worry about it. Fame might suck, but it's worth it.

Of course, if you're already signed to a particular record company or a publisher, you should always consult them first as they might have a rather different view from yours.

Getting Extra Money

Aside from the advances and/or royalties that you'll get from record and publishing deals and the money you make from selling your own records yourself, there are a few other sources of cash that are very handy. The sting about these is that, even if the money has been collected and is there waiting, you'll never get it if you don't know where to look.

Copyright is the thing that record company and publishers' contracts are all about: the ownership of the right to make copies (records) of the music and sell them. Once you sign a deal, you lose the power to deal with your own copyright because you've sold it to the company.

Performing rights, however, almost always stay with you and carry on making money for you for years afterwards, even if you have never agreed anything with anyone or signed up to any organisations or have never heard of them. Performing rights were invented and granted by the government (just as copyright was) to protect songwriters and musical performers from unpaid exploitation. The government actually wants musicians and songwriters to be paid for every single performance they give, whether live or recorded.

Live performances are the easiest to protect. If a musician is to give a live performance and wishes to be paid for it, he can easily protect himself by refusing to perform without getting paid – simple and effective, and no need for the government's help. But what about recorded performances?

Every single time a restaurant or a bar that has a stereo system plays your record to its customers, you, as the musical artist, are giving a recorded performance and you are getting paid for it. If the record is on a jukebox, the system is straightforward because we all know that every play of a jukebox record requires a payment from the audience, and the jukebox company can hardly hide the fact that it plays your record. But there aren't many jukeboxes around any more.

Owners of every restaurant, bar, cinema, shop, grocery store, airport, doctor's and dentist's office, telephone's 'on hold' system and elevator has to pay in order to legally play music to its captive audience of customers, and the musicians and songwriters who made the music get the money. In the UK, the licence system is run through a single government-sanctioned organisation called the PRS (Performing Right Society) and every establishment must deal with them and pay regular fees to them in order to get a licence. (The US counterpart is SESAC.) The PRS, in turn, pays the money on to its members – all of whom are the songwriters of tunes which are released in the UK. Money is also distributed to the musicians who performed on the records by a society called the PPL (Phonographic Performance Ltd).

Further money is paid to the performing musicians and artists for plays of their records on TV and radio, partly through the PRS and PPL and partly by PAMRA (Performing Arts Media Rights Association), VPL (Video Performance Ltd) and the Musicians' Union. These organisations monitor the playlists of many UK outlets and use this information to create weekly, monthly and annual lists of which records are being played by whom to what audience, and from these lists they make a division of the money collected and (here's the best part) send cheques directly to the homes of the songwriters and musicians, regardless of whether they have signed record and publishing deals or not. Money goes to the original composers of the tune and anyone who plays on the record, including the band members themselves, any featured artists and also session players, studio musicians or extra performers who were uncredited on the sleeve.

In the UK, it is necessary, however, for every person who has ever written or played (including any programming of computers and sequencers for dance music) on a record that has been released in the UK, and is likely to have or have had in the past any such plays, to join each of these organisations personally and give them details of the relevant records and their address for posting the cash. The details of the organisations can be easily found on-line (and if you find any one of them then ask them for the others, they will happily give you all the details to save you from multiple searches).

Unbelievably, even when you play a record to

yourself at home, the government has found a way to collect money for it and pay it to the musicians. This is done via the extra bit of tax you pay whenever you purchase blank tapes in the UK (it's called a 'levy'), and it's distributed as described above.

It's amazing to discover each year just how often your record is still being played by someone somewhere and therefore generating a bit of income, even years after it has disappeared from the charts. It's even more amazing that it's never too late to join these organisations, as they can – and do – send out back-pay.

Contracts

Be wary of contracts offered for you to sign. Most contracts that get bandied about in the music business are unnecessary – especially if they only create a relationship between an artist and a manager or a production company without any cash changing hands.

There is very often no need for a written contract between a hopeful DJ/artist and his manager – and especially not before the time when a record deal is offered and accepted. If a manager is really appropriate for an artist, a huge measure of trust must exist between them. Furthermore, almost any offer of a deal from a record company will be based on the fact – and will require – that the artist retains that manager. This is because the deal will depend in huge measure on the manager's skill in guiding the artist through the process of development from hopeful to hitman.

Most contracts with production companies are unnecessary, at least in the first instance. As with

Carl Cox (right), the biggest DJ in the UK, together with Point Blank's Rob Cowan

managers, the ability of a production company to steer a tune from the studio to the chart is equally dependent on the artist and the business acumen of the production company. The artist knows that, if he pulls out of the deal with the production company in midstream, the likelihood of success falls, and the production company knows that, if they stuff the artist at any point, everyone loses.

Of course, few people will ever part with dosh without having signed something. So, if money's involved – such as an advance or stumping-up for large expenses – there may be no avoiding a contract.

If you're ever faced with a contract written in lawyerese (and they all are), think carefully before paying for legal advice. There's no sense in paying out £1,000 to a lawyer for advice about a contract worth only £2,000. Start by asking the person who has offered you the contract to rewrite it in plain English (it's surprising how often people will do this without a complaint or a grudge). Contracts in any language are as worthy as those written in any other language, as long as they can be read and clearly understood by both parties. If the request for rewriting in plain English is denied, ask them to explain the contract to you in writing. Anything in writing which attempts to explain the contract as either or both of the parties sees it will actually form part of the contract (unless it says specifically that it doesn't), and you can rely on that explanation if it's clearly understandable.

Finally, if and when the time comes to hire a lawyer, make sure you get an estimate of how much the advice is going to cost (plus extras) and tell them to let you know in writing before it goes over the estimate.

A top DJ at the Ministry Of Sound

10 OUTRO

'If you get stopped at Customs with your records and they ask to see your work visa, explain that you are spending a few days away with your partner and that these are the records you make love to. Worked for me.' *Daft Fader, producer and DJ*

Well, now that you know everything there is to know about DJing, what are you going to do? A world of clubs is waiting for you out there.

Reading this book might have been the start of it all for you, or it might have been a handy refresher course. It might even have been just a top-up to a lifetime of skills already mastered. Wherever you now sit in the grand scheme of DJing, there is always one good option for the next step: practise harder.

As with any skill in life, the more you do it, the better you become, and DJing is no exception. Bedroom practice will improve your basic skills, experimentation will expand your knowledge and help you find those elusive records that together form the perfect mix, while playing out (anywhere at all) will always improve your audience-reading ability.

We end where we began – the goal and the means:

- The goal is an audience;
- The means is practice, practice, practice.

Happy DJing!

GLOSSARY

12-inch
In the 1980s, this term meant an extended mix of a single song, but it now simply refers to a vinyl record.

A Cappella
A version of a song with all the instruments removed, leaving only the vocals (singing, rapping or speaking).

AFL
After Fader Level, a button on the mixer that, when pressed, allows only the sound in the corresponding channel to be heard, either through the speakers or the headphones only. The opposite to PFL.

Ambient
1) A genre of music using big, swirly sounds and long introductions or 2) the incidental noises or sounds in any given situation.

Amplifier
The box that provides the power with which the speakers are driven.

Audio Clip
A snippet of previously recorded sound, typically a few beats of a drum pattern or a recorded word of speech.

Aux Input
Often found on amplifiers and mixers, this refers to an input for an auxiliary device such as a CD player, MiniDisc and so on.

Awsy
A top bloke who anyone who is anyone in Ibiza knows.

Back-To-Back Mixing
When one DJ follows another to continue the mix.

Bass
The lower-range sounds audible to the human ear, including the string bass, the electric bass, the bass drum, the lower strings of a cello, the lower notes of a piano, a tuba, a baritone singer and so on.

Bass Line
A pattern of low-range notes played on a string bass, an electric bass or a synthesiser.

Battle
When two or more DJs use their music to compete against each other.

Beat Juggling
The act of making a new drum pattern from two records by playing them slightly out of synchronisation.

Beat Mixing
The act of locking beats from two different tracks together in synchronisation.

Belt Drive
A type of traditional turntable which uses a belt as a gear chain via which the motor spins the platter.

Binary Code
The language used by computers, made of 1s and 0s

Blagger
Someone who wants things for free.

Bling

Technically refers to over-the-top ladies' jewellery but is often used as an appreciation of something good.

Bo

Exclamation of encouragement to a DJ or a mark of approval.

Box Boy

A person who is employed to carry record boxes from the car to the DJ box.

BPM

Beats per minute, a measure of the speed of a song or, literally, the number of musical beats that occur in a song during one minute.

Breakdown

A section of a song in which most of the instruments drop out or stop playing, leaving, typically, only one or two drums carrying on the beat or, less typically, only one or two ambient instruments playing.

Cans

Slang for headphones.

Cartridge

A stylus (often called a needle).

Club

A venue for music and dancing.

Composer

The writer of a song or other piece of music.

Controller

A device used to manipulate computer-based sound files.

Crash

Occurs when a DJ attempts to mix two tunes and fails.

Crossfader

A horizontal slider switch found on mixers to enable audio to be quickly shifted from one source to another.

Cubase

A computer music program developed by Steinberg and available commercially for both PC and Mac.

Cue Point

A useful point on a track that can be easily returned to, such as the first beat of the track.

Cueing

Physically moving the record to find a desired point – ie the first beat.

Cymbal Crash

Usually marks the beginning of a new musical phrase. Can be used to phrase-match two records.

Deck

Slang for turntable.

Delay

A quick or short echo of a sound.

Demo CD

A recording of a DJ's mix burnt onto CD and used as a demonstration of his mixing abilities and to market the DJ for gigs

Denon

Manufacturer of DJ hardware.

Digital Mixing

Mixing music that is stored as a computer file, ie MP3 or .WAV.

Direct Drive

A type of traditional turntable in which the motor turns the platter directly, without any intervening mechanism.

Disc

Slang term for vinyl record, CD or computer storage medium.

DJ Box

The place in a club where you will find the play-out equipment (decks, mixer and so on).

Effects
Refers to any or all of the electronic boxes or software programs that artificially create echo, reverb, phasing or any of the other usual special effects found in dance music.

Emcee
A person who uses a microphone to add lyrics to tracks.

EQ/Equaliser
An electronic device for adjusting the frequency response of sound.

Fade
To slowly and gently remove the sound from the mix.

Fader
The proper word for slider, the up-and-down control on a mixer.

Fill
A short drum pattern that marks the end of a phrase.

Flier
An advert for an event that is often handed out during other events.

Flight Case
Alloy case used to protect equipment during transit.

Flip Side
The reverse or B-side of a record.

Frequency
A sliver of sound within the range of human hearing, typically along the lines of 'treble', 'bass' or '1kHz'.

Groove
The imprint on a record that guides the stylus.

Hamster Switch
See *Crossfader*.

Hard Drive
A mechanical mass-storage device for computers.

Having It Right Out
Partying very hard for a duration of time.

Headphones
Those things that keep your ears warm and have little speakers in them so you can hear the music privately.

Hi-hat
A pair of inverted cymbals played by a drummer.

Hook
The part of a song that you remember.

Ibiza
A small island off the coast of Spain that is the undisputed party capital of the world.

Instrumental
A part of music or, more commonly, a whole track that has no vocal.

Internet
The place to download music and other things.

Jack
An audio connector, typically a quarter-inch plug.

Jewel Box
Plastic protective case for CDs.

Jumping
When the needle won't stay in the groove of the record, or when the whole dance floor is dancing excitedly to your selection of music.

Kettle Lead
A mains power lead that has a connector at one end the same as those found on electric kettles.

Key
The chosen register for a song.

Keyboard
Refers to either the QWERTY typewriter keyboard for a computer or the keys of a piano or synthesiser.

Kick Drum
The biggest drum in a kit, which sits on the floor and is played by a drummer using a pedal beater.

Label (Area)
The paper-covered centre circle on a vinyl record.

Leads
Wires with plugs on the end to connect electrical devices and audio equipment.

Line
As in Phono/Line. A line input is used for CD players and just about any signal sending separate, other than decks, which have a phono input (as in phonographic).

Locked
When two records are in perfect bpm synchronisation.

Looping
Repeating a section of music over and over again.

Mac
Short for Macintosh, a computer made by Apple. (Popularly, the other kind of computer from the PC.)

Mains
The wall socket supply.

Master Fader
The fader that turns the whole volume down. Usually found on the right-hand side of the mixer.

Master Output
A control that affects the overall audio output.

Meter
A visual device displaying audio levels.

Mid Range
The sounds, audible to the human ear, which are neither bass nor treble.

MIDI
Musical Instrument Digital Interface – the computer language for music, in which every parameter is represented by a number.

Mingin'
Unattractive or malodorous.

Mix
'In the mix' during the act of beat mixing.

Mixer
The device that sits between the two audio sources to enable manipulation of audio signals

MP3
A computer file format used for storing music.

Ms
Abbreviation of millisecond, one-thousandth of a second.

Mute
To remove all audio.

Needle
The tip at the end of the cartridge that reads the music information in the record grooves. Also known as a stylus.

Numark
Manufacturer of DJ equipment.

Oggy Oggy Oggy
A favourite line for emcees to shout when they want some audience participation.

On-line
Describes when one is connected to the Internet.

Ortofon
A stylus manufacturer.

Panning
The shifting of sound between right and left within the stereo spectrum.

PC
Personal computer (not a Mac).

PFL
Pre-Fader Listen, a switch that enables you to listen to the audio pre (ie before it goes out through) the fader, for the audience to hear. Opposite to AFL.

Phasing
The sound effect which occurs when the same sound is played almost exactly against itself, but not quite.

Phono/Line switch
A switch that enables one mixer channel to share two types of input.

Phrase
A 'sentence' of music, usually 4, 8, 16 or 32 bars long.

Pitch Adjustment/Shifter/Controller
A sliding control found on a turntable that enables the user to change the pitch of a track and, in turn, the bpm.

Pitch Shifting
Changing the bpm of a track.

Platter
The flat, round, spinning platform on a turntable on which the record rests.

Playa
Someone who never sold out.

Portastudio
A tape-based home recording studio.

Power Cable
The lead connecting a machine to the wall socket.

Practice
The thing we all must do, as often as possible.

Producing
The act of directing the making of a record.

Promo
A record that a DJ gets prior to a general public release.

Promotion
Actively putting forward a product or an idea.

Publisher
A person or company which pays a writer for the privilege of 'owning' or 'administering' his compositions.

Quantise
Aka 'auto-correct', the process by which a computer or sequencer corrects the mistakes in a musical performance, thereby making it 'perfect'.

Raver
A person who frequents clubs on a regular basis.

Reaction Sheet
A feedback form filled in by DJs.

Record Company
An entity that actually distributes and markets records.

Record Label
A sub-division of a record company.

Recording
The act of capturing a musical performance (via computer or tape).

Reverb
The splash of sound which derives from a noise occurring in an enclosed area.

Rewind
Often shouted by happy clubbers who want to hear the track again.

Rider
A list of wants made available at a venue for the DJ.

Rinsin'
Descriptive word for a top tune.

Ripping
The act of loading music from a source CD to a computer-based storage medium.

Roland
Music hardware and software manufacturer.

Sample
An audio clip – a small snippet of sound captured and manipulated for use on a subsequent record.

Sampler
A digital recorder which captures short snippets of sound, usually from other pre-existing records

Scratching
The manipulation of snippets of sound to produce effects.

Sennheiser
Manufacturer of audio equipment.

Sleeve
Paper of plastic protective layer for vinyl records.

Slider
Colloquial word for fader.

Slipmat
Sits between the record and the platter to enable the record to spin freely.

Snare Drum
On a drum kit, the drum which sits virtually in the drummer's lap and has wires strung across the bottom to create a fizz when struck. The snare drum provides the backbeat in dance music

Songwriter
The actual composer of a song.

Sound System
A complete amplified speaker set-up.

Source (Material)
Relates to the audio.

Source Machine
Relates to the device that plays audio.

Spangled
Describes someone who is in no fit state.

Spin Back
To spin back a record on the turntable.

Spindle
A short metal rod found in the middle of the turntable platter that slips into the hole in the record.

Stanton
Manufacturer of styli and the mighty Final Scratch digital playout system.

Static
Unwanted electrical charge.

Stereo
The system of playing back recorded music in which different sounds come out of each of two speakers, thereby recreating the effect of hearing a band 'live' on stage.

Stylus
See *Needle*.

SWITCH
Also known as knob, something that can be turned or thrown in order to change the setting of a piece of equipment.

Switch52
A company that specialises in building digital playout systems for DJs.

Synchronise
To make two things appear as in line.

Synth
Short for synthesiser, an electronic machine (or computer-based software) that makes musical noises or sounds to play with.

Technics
Manufacturer of industry-standard turntables.

Tempo

The speed of a piece of music, expressed in bpm.

Tonality

The overall sound or key of a piece of music.

Tone Arm

Found on a deck, this is the device that tracks the stylus across the record.

Tone Control

The ability to change the frequency response of sound, usually by adjusting treble, bass, mids, etc.

Treble

The higher-ranged sounds audible to the human ear, typically violins, upper notes of a piano, cymbals, the sound of the letter S, etc.

Tune

A song.

Turntable

Or deck – an audio device that plays records.

Venue

A place of social events in which to do gigs.

Vestax

Hardware manufacturer of turntables and quality mixers.

VIP

Abbreviation for Very Important Person. Many clubs have a VIP bar that is generally reserved for people who don't use public transport

VU Meter

The jumping needle seen in studios and on mixers.

WAV/.WAV

Music stored on a computer without any compression

Wave Cycle

The undulating movement of sound through air.

White Label

Refers to a pre-release record. The centre label is white, with the title and artist hand-written.

Zero Position

The 'null' of a control when it is 'set to zero'.

Zonked

When you are truly exhausted and can physically take no more.

NOTES